THEORIES OF EDUCATIONAL MANAGEMENT

The Author

Tony Bush is a senior lecturer in educational policy and management at the Open University. He was formerly a teacher in secondary schools and a college of higher education and a professional officer with a local education authority. He has written and edited a number of books and articles on aspects of policy making and management in education.

THEORIES OF EDUCATIONAL MANAGEMENT

Tony Bush

The Open University

P·C·P
Paul Chapman
Publishing Ltd

First published 1986
Harper & Row Ltd
London

Reprinted by
Paul Chapman Publishing Ltd
144 Liverpool Road
London N1 1LA

British Library Cataloguing in Publication Data

Bush, T
    Theories of educational management
    I. Schools, management and organization
    I. Theories of educational management
    371.2′001   LB2805

    ISBN 1-85396-041-1

Typeset by Inforum Ltd, Portsmouth
Printed and bound in Great Britain by
Athenaeum Press Ltd, Newcastle upon tyne

C D E F G 4 3 2 1

CONTENTS

PREFACE

There is a developing awareness of the importance of good management for the effective operation of schools and colleges. The larger institutions have hundreds of staff, thousands of students and budgets which run to several million pounds. Good management is regarded as essential if these resources are to be deployed to maximum effect. More significant, however, is the importance of effective management for the pupils and students in educational institutions of all sizes. Their future opportunities depend to a considerable extent on the quality of the educational experience offered in the primary and secondary schools they attend. Many factors contribute to differences between educational institutions but there is evidence that the nature and style of management are central considerations in distinguishing between successful and less successful schools.

A literature on management *practice* in educational organizations is developing in response to the establishment of the many new courses on educational management. However, there have been few attempts to address the theoretical foundations of good practice. The aim of this book is to provide some conceptual frameworks to set alongside the essentially practical orientation of many of the new courses. The theories are linked to examples of practice in primary and secondary schools and in colleges. The book seeks to present a complex body of theory in clear, straightforward terms and to illustrate concepts by reference to situations and events in educational institutions. In making relevant theory more accessible to practitioners the intention is to promote a greater understanding of the managerial problems they encounter in their daily work.

Chapter 1 defines educational management and stresses the significance of purposes or goals to institutional management. There is discussion about whether education is a special case justifying a distinct approach to the training of school and college managers. The emphasis here, and throughout the book, is on the management of educational organizations rather than the wider educational system.

Chapter 2 considers the relationship between theory and practice. It is suggested that theories and concepts provide the framework for managerial decision-making. The various perspectives emphasize different aspects of organizations but they tend to be both normative and selective and these characteristics are discussed here.

The next five chapters are the heart of the book, each presenting one of the major models of educational management. The five perspectives are analyzed in terms of the assumptions made about the goals of educational institutions, the nature of organizational structure, relations with the external environment and the most appropriate styles of leadership.

Chapter 3 considers formal models, with their emphasis on hierarchical structures, rational processes and official authority. Chapter 4 outlines democratic models which stress the authority of expertise, the shared values and objectives of professional staff and decision-making based on consensus. Chapter 5 presents political models with their assumptions of conflict between interest groups and decisions dependent on the relative resources of power deployed by the various factions. Chapter 6 examines subjective models with their accent on the individual interpretation of events and their rejection of the concept of organizational goals. Chapter 7 discusses ambiguity models which emphasize the unpredictability of organizations, the lack of clarity about goals and the fluid nature of participation in decision-making.

Chapter 8 compares the five models and considers their validity for particular types of school or college. The chapter concludes with a consideration of several attempts to integrate some of the models.

I am indebted to Professor Tony Becher of Sussex University and Professor Ron Glatter of the Open University for their constructive comments on a draft of this text. Helen Knowles has typed successive drafts of the manuscript and assisted with the administration of the project.

Tony Bush

CHAPTER 1

THE IMPORTANCE OF MANAGEMENT FOR EDUCATION

What is educational management?

Educational management is a field of study and practice concerned with the operation of educational organizations. There is no single generally accepted definition of the subject because its development has drawn heavily on several more firmly established disciplines including sociology, political science and economics. As Harries-Jenkins (1984) suggests, 'we are looking at a field of management studies characterized by a considerable flexibility of discipline boundaries'. Interpretations drawn from different disciplines necessarily emphasize rather different aspects of educational management and these varying approaches are reflected in subsequent chapters of this book.

Many of the definitions of educational management which have been offered by writers are *partial* because they reflect the particular stance of the author. Those which attempt a broader approach are often rather bland. Hoyle (1981, p. 8), for example, describes his definition as 'downbeat':

> Management is a continuous process through which members of an organisation seek to co-ordinate their activities and utilise their resources in order to fulfil the various tasks of the organisation as efficiently as possible.

Cuthbert (1984) suggests that management 'is an activity involving responsibility for getting things done through other people'.

Glatter's (1979, p. 16) definition is useful because it serves to identify the scope of the subject. He argues that management studies are concerned with:

> [. . .] the internal operation of educational institutions, and also with their relationships with their environments, that is, the communities in which they are set, and with the governing bodies to which they are formally responsible.

This statement delineates the boundaries of educational management but leaves open questions about the nature of the subject. What are those issues which are centrally the concern of a managerial approach to schools and colleges? Arguably, educational management has at its heart matters concerned with the purposes or aims of education.

Most writers on educational management emphasize the significance of purposes or goals in education. Culbertson (1983), for example, claims that 'defining purpose is a central function of administration'. Cyert (1975) argues that 'an organisation is developed to achieve certain goals or objectives by group activity'. The centrality of the goal orientation of schools and colleges is common to most of the different theoretical approaches to the subject. There is disagreement, though, about the value of *formal* statements of purpose, about *whose* purposes may become the objectives of the organization and about *how* the institution's goals are determined.

The formal aims of schools and colleges tend to be set at a high level of generality. They usually command substantial support but, because they are often utopian, such objectives provide an inadequate basis for managerial action. A typical aim in a primary or secondary school might focus on the acquisition by each pupil of physical, social, intellectual and moral qualities and skills. This is worthy but it has considerable limitations as a guide to decision-making. More specific purposes often fail to reach the same level of agreement. A proposal to seek an improved record in public examinations, for example, might be challenged by teachers concerned about the implications for pupils in non-examination groups.

Certain approaches to educational management are concerned predominantly with *organizational* objectives while other models strongly emphasize *individual* aims. There is a range of opinion between these two views. Gray (1979, p. 12), for example, suggests that:

> [. . .] the management process is concerned with helping the members of an organisation to attain individual as well as organisational objectives within the changing environment of the organisation.

It may be that individual and organizational objectives are incompatible or that organizational aims satisfy some, but not all, individual aspirations. It can be assumed that most teachers want their school or college to pursue policies which are in harmony with their own interests and preferences.

Certainly Coulson (1985) is right to assert that 'the goals and motivations of all the individuals involved in the life of the school interpenetrate with the goals officially attributed to the organisation'.

The headteacher is particularly well placed to promote his own objectives as the aims of the school. Poster (1976) asserts that 'it is [the head] who will determine the priorities of management'. In many schools and colleges, however, goal setting is a corporate activity undertaken by formal bodies or informal groups. The nature of the goal-setting process is a major element in the different models of educational management to be discussed in subsequent chapters.

The origins and development of educational management as a field of study have been well chronicled by Culbertson (1980), Bone (1982) and Hughes (1984). It began in the United States in the early part of this century. Development in the United Kingdom came as late as the 1960s but there has been rapid expansion since then and by 1981 there were 1600 students on award-bearing courses at 58 institutions. There were also 20 000 students on non award-bearing courses (Hughes et al. 1981). In 1983 the Department of Education and Science (DES) sponsored a programme of management training for heads and established the National Development Centre for School Management Training at Bristol University to monitor provision. The Open University Advanced Diploma in Educational Management attracted 2300 students in 1985 alone.

The growth of the subject reflects the view that the management of educational institutions is enhanced by training just as teachers require training to be effective in the classroom. The content and nature of training for educational management is more contentious. In particular there is disagreement about whether the management of education is different from the management of other organizations.

The significance of the educational context

One strand of opinion asserts that there are general principles of management which can be applied to all organizational settings. Handy (1984) claims that schools 'have much in common with other organisations that bring people together for a purpose – be they hospitals, or businesses or government offices'. Haag (1982) dismisses the idea that education requires separate treatment. He concludes that 'the assertion that every enterprise represents a unique case which calls for its own solution is without foundation and contradicted by the facts'. Walker (1984) advocates common management education for administrators from government, business and education. He believes that 'these men and woman learn from one another in a process of managerial symbiosis'.

The case for a common approach to the education of managers rests largely upon the functions thought to be common to different types of organization. These include financial management, personnel management and relationships with the organization's clients and the wider community. Yet many would argue that educational institutions have several special features which justify a distinct approach to the training of those charged with running our schools and colleges.

The majority view among academics and practitioners is that the management of educational institutions is sufficiently different to merit separate provision for the education and training of school and college managers. Glatter (1972) claims that 'educational institutions differ along crucial dimensions from other kinds of organisations'. Barrell (1982, p. 6) points to the views held by many people inside schools and colleges.

> Teachers [. . .] are often impatient when they hear about line management in schools. They see it as an inappropriate attempt to introduce industrial techniques into a situation which is based on personal relationships. Education, they say, is not susceptible to the imposition of hard-headed business concepts designed to increase profit margins.

Taylor (1976) is one academic who has been cautious about the increasing emphasis on management within education. 'Prominent among such objections is that management theory and practice have been developed mainly in connection with industrial and commercial activities, which are seen as intrinsically different from the activities of educational institutions.' Greenfield (1973, p. 561) has been a persistent critic of management and organizational theory and his views receive extensive treatment in Chapter 6. One strand of his argument concerns the inapplicability of general organizational theory to educational institutions:

> [. . .] we should be more careful than we usually are about making prescriptions for organisational change that assume similar dynamics in the operation of most, if not all, organisations. Prescriptive organisation theory [. . .] is often based almost exclusively upon study of economic organisations; one seldom gets the feeling that prescriptions for educational change are based upon theories and conceptions of *schools*.

Culbertson (1980, p. 327) asserts:

> [. . .] scholars are questioning the fruitfulness of building or relying upon general theories of administration [. . .] Such an orientation, they argue,

leads inevitably to the neglect of educational purpose and practice and the special features of leadership and change in educational institutions.

It is clear that many writers consider that education requires special treatment because schools and colleges possess many distinctive characteristics.

There are six major areas in which the management of educational institutions differs markedly from the management of other organizations:

1. The *objectives* of educational institutions are much more difficult to define than the purposes of commercial organizations. There are no clear-cut educational equivalents to such major private sector objectives as profit maximization, output maximization or product diversification. Schools and colleges are expected to develop the personal capacity of individuals, to inculcate the accepted values and beliefs, to look after children and young people for set periods of each day and to prepare pupils and students for the next stage of education, for employment or, increasingly, for unemployment. These are ambitious targets which are often in conflict. The teacher is expected to be the social worker, the custodian and the quasi-parent as well as developing the pupil's capacity to learn. The ordering of priorities within this complex set of objectives is fraught with difficulties.

2. It is very difficult to *measure* whether or not objectives have been achieved in education. In commercial organizations it is possible to measure success in financial terms – sales have increased, profits are up, dividends are higher. Several factors militate against such straightforward evaluations in schools and colleges. Any assessment has to be long term to allow for the sheer length of the educational process – a minimum of eleven years for every citizen and several years more for a significant minority. Even then certain aspects cannot be adequately measured. How do you assess the adequacy of socialization or the extent of individual development? It is possible to measure the results of public examinations and to test literacy and numeracy. Yet there is a danger that educational institutions will be assessed only in such terms while the more elusive criteria are undervalued or overlooked. As Handy (1984, p. 21) suggests, the absence of acceptable bases for evaluation creates serious management difficulties.

> Faced with blurred aims, conflicting functions and no simple way of measuring success, schools have a major management problem. Without clear and agreed objectives there are no criteria for deciding how to allocate resources – everything becomes a political debate about priorities. Without clear measures of success there are no obvious ways to assess the progress of individuals and departments – every judgement is subjective and personal.

3. The presence of *children* and young people as the focal points of educational institutions leads to additional sources of ambiguity. Pupils and students may be regarded as clients or outputs of schools and colleges. As clients there are unique characteristics which are explored below. As participants in a production process young people differ markedly from the raw material of industry and commerce. Children cannot be processed, programmed or manipulated. The learning process is built on personal relationships with all the idiosyncracy and unpredictability that implies. This human variability reinforces the problems of measurement discussed earlier.

4. The managers and teachers in schools (and to a lesser extent colleges) are from a common *professional* background with shared values, training and experience. As professionals, teachers claim a measure of autonomy in the teaching and learning process. The nature of the relationship with the class or group is not amenable to close definition or supervision. It suggests also that teachers should be able to participate in school or college decision-making because their commitment to the implementation of decisions is essential if the decision-making process is to be more than an empty ritual. The 'client' relationship between teacher and student differs in several respects from other professional–client links. Teachers have regular and extended contact with pupils; often several encounters a week for a period of years. Moreover, pupils have little opportunity to select their teachers. Children are required to spend at least eleven years as members of educational institutions and to accept that their teachers will be chosen for them. Glatter (1972, p. 8) emphasizes that this is another unique aspect of educational institutions which necessarily influences their management:

> This gives organisational problems in schools, and to only a slightly lesser degree in most other types of educational institution . . . a fundamentally different character from those of nearly every other form of institution, even those which employ a high proportion of professional workers.

5. There is a *fragmented* organizational and management structure both within and impinging upon educational institutions. The climate for school and college decision-making is strongly influenced by a plethora of external agencies and groups. These include politicians, officials and inspectors at national and local levels as well as parents and both formal and *ad hoc* pressure groups. Inside institutions there are multiple decision points concerning the management of the school or college and its sub-units – departments, faculties, houses and years. This fragmentation makes it

difficult to locate responsibility for management decision-making in schools and colleges.

6. Many of the senior and middle managers in schools, and to a lesser extent colleges, have *little time* for the managerial aspects of their work. In primary schools most or all staff are full-time class teachers. Only the head has significant opportunities to engage in managerial activity and in smaller schools the head teaches on a full-time or part-time basis. In secondary schools the head may be free of teaching commitments while deputies typically teach a 50 per cent timetable (Bush, 1981). Other staff have a heavy teaching load and managerial activities are squeezed into the limited 'free' time. This time limitation has serious implications for the nature of management in educational institutions with decision-making often reverting simply to those who are available.

The special characteristics of educational institutions imply caution in the application of management models or practices drawn from non-educational settings. Of course all organizations have common features but the distinctive qualities of schools and colleges limit the validity of approaches borrowed from industrial or commercial bodies. As Baldridge *et al.* (1978, p. 9) recommend, careful evaluation and adaptation of such models is required before they can be applied with confidence to educational organizations.

> [. . .] traditional management theories cannot be applied to educational institutions without carefully considering whether they will work well in that unique academic setting [. . .] We therefore must be extremely careful about attempts to manage or improve [. . .] education with 'modern management' techniques borrowed from business, for example. Such borrowing may make sense, but it must be approached very carefully.

Managers and professionals

Schools and colleges are staffed predominantly by professionals. This has implications for the nature of management in educational institutions because professionals seek a measure of control over their working environment. As Handy (1984) suggests, schools are 'organisations of professionals who, in the manner of professionals, like to manage themselves'. In practice, however, teachers are usually too busy with their pedagogic activities to be able to devote much of their time to management. Many of the major management responsibilities are exercised on their behalf, often by the head or principal. This may be acceptable to teachers as long as the managers are drawn from their own professional background. As a result almost all heads are successful teachers who have credibility within the profession and value their background as practitioners. Hughes (1984) shows that 'heads [. . .] still regard themselves first and foremost as head *teachers*, not as managers or administrators'.

There are significant difficulties in sustaining aspects of professionalism when staff are employed on a salaried basis within organizations. The key client relationship is mediated by organizational variables and cannot be on an individual basis as in many professional–client encounters. However, teachers do have expertise and common values derived from their training. They are also granted a high degree of autonomy in their classroom work. Perhaps above all they have that commitment to their pupils and students which is the hallmark of any profession. Culbertson (1983, p. 18) describes this quality as a moral commitment:

> The first great commitment, professional responsibility, is developed when practitioners acquire the attitude that they are a part of their clients and that they will know, live with, and suffer the consequences of their professional decisions.

The management of professionals cannot be based simply on a bureaucratic structure but has to acknowledge the expertise of teachers as individuals, and as a group of staff within an institution. The integrating force between the needs of the organization and the expectations of the teachers is provided by the head, who is often sandwiched uncomfortably between the conflicting pressures of bureaucracy and professionalism. Hughes (1976) has developed a 'professional as administrator' model which encompasses the head's dual role as the chief executive of a school and the leading professional within it. As chief executive heads are accountable to external bodies for the successful management of the institution. As leading professional they are responsible for the leadership of a group of teachers. Hughes (1976, p. 60) concludes:

> [. . .] the professional as administrator fulfils his mediating role to a large extent by providing the kind of supervision of professional staff and the kind of organisational leadership in responding to external change, which is acceptable to professionals.

Effective management in a hostile climate

The management of educational institutions in the 1980s is beset with problems. The 30 per cent decline in the birth rate between 1964 and 1977 has produced a sharp fall in the populations of many schools and resulted in the closure of some. Schools and colleges also face lower levels of funding which necessarily affect the standard and quality of the service they provide. Teachers are also responsible for the development of young people at a time of serious economic difficulties. The world of employment is unattainable for many of the clients of schools, particularly in the depressed inner cities. These developments have occurred as teachers experience reductions in pay, promotion opportunities and self-esteem. For all these reasons educational institutions now provide a searching test of managerial competence.

The issues and problems facing schools and colleges illustrate their increasing dependence on the environment. Writing in 1978, and with particular reference to higher education, Baldridge *et al.* (pp. 24–25) chart the growing vulnerability of educational institutions to external variables.

> All complex organisations are vulnerable to outside pressure; there is simply no completely 'independent' or 'autonomous' organisation. But they vary a great deal on how much the outside world controls them, with some institutions having considerably more freedom of action than others. The degree of autonomy that an organisation has in regard to its environment is one of the critical determinants of how it will be managed. [. . .] Although colleges and universities are not entirely captured by their environments, they are steadily being penetrated by outside forces. As this vulnerability grows, the institutions change significantly in their management patterns.

In Britain these environmental pressures have intensified since 1978 and arguably affect schools even more than higher education. Carlson (1975, p. 191) distinguishes between 'wild' and 'domesticated' organizations in assessing their dependence on the environment. He suggests that domestic organizations are protected from their environment.

> There is no struggle for survival for this type of organisation. Like the domesticated animal, these organisations are fed and cared for. Existence is guaranteed. Though their type of organisation does compete in a restricted area for funds, funds are not closely tied to quality of performance. These organisations are domesticated in the sense that they are protected by the society they serve.

Carlson contrasts domesticated organizations with wild organizations, which:

> [. . .] do struggle for survival. Their existence is not guaranteed, and they do cease to exist. Support for them is closely tied to quality of performance, and a steady flow of clients is not assured. Wild organizations are not protected at vulnerable points as are domesticated organizations.

Schools and higher education institutions (but not further education colleges) might have been regarded as 'domesticated' until the demographic and economic pressures of the 1980s. Now schools in particular are exhibiting many of the characteristics of 'wild' organizations, as Glatter (1984, pp. 9–10) makes clear:

> There has been a general shift towards 'wildness' throughout education, including the school sector, as closures have become common and survival has become problematic, and as institutions have found it necessary to supplement their income from non-traditional sources.

The impact of environmental pressures on the nature and style of management will be discussed at length in subsequent chapters of this book but three major effects can be noted here:

1. The continuing uncertainty over levels of funding and the supply of clients leads to an emphasis on decision-making for the *short-term*. Planning horizons are reduced because managers simply cannot assess staffing levels, pupil or student numbers or the finance available for equipment or to support innovation. Resources in schools (and to a lesser extent in colleges) are tied closely to pupil numbers. For 'wild' organizations in particular staffing and curriculum may be subject to change according to the size of the next intake of pupils. For many managers there is limited value in planning beyond this point.
2. The management of schools and colleges is dominated by *resource issues*. Heads and principals spend much of their time on the organization and distribution of resources, often just to meet existing commitments. Increasingly institutions are dependent upon unofficial sources of funds, such as parents and industry. This may in turn lead to greater accountability to these groups with further implications for the nature of institutional management.
3. The increasing vulnerability of schools and colleges to environmental pressures may lead to decision-making being *drawn to the centre* of many institutions. Teachers who have responsibility for relationships with the major external bodies and groups may be able to influence decisions by virtue of their control over these communication networks. Heads and principals often have the prime responsibility for external links and their ability to interpret external pressures may serve to increase their power within the institution.

As environmental pressures intensify so managers require greater skill and resilience to sustain their institutions, as Culbertson (1980, p. 329) demonstrates:

In countries beset by decline, the professional development of leaders is seen more and more as an important strategy for helping organisations achieve renewal and, in turn, for attaining greater efficiency and effectiveness in education.

References

Baldridge, J.V., Curtis, D.V., Ecker, G. and Riley, G.L. (1978) *Policy-Making and Effective Leadership*, Jossey Bass, San Francisco

Barrell, G. (1982) Accountability in school management, *Education Today*, Vol. 32, No. 2, pp 3–8 *Education Today* is the Journal of the College of Preceptors

Bone, T.R. (1982) Educational administration. *British Journal of Educational Studies*, Vol. 30, No. 1, pp 32–42

Bush, T. (1981) *Key Roles in School Management*, E323 Management and the School, Block 4, Part 3, The Open University Press, Milton Keynes

Carlson, R.O. (1975) Environmental constraints and organisational consequences: the Public School and its Clients. In J.V. Baldridge and T.E. Deal (Eds.) *Managing Change in Educational Organisations*, McCutchan, Berkeley, © 1975 by McCutchan Publishing Corporation, Berkeley, CA

Coulson, A. (1985) *The Managerial Behaviour of Primary School Heads*, Collected Original Resources in Education, Carfax Publishing Company, Abingdon

Culbertson, J. (1978) *Educational Administration: where we are and where we are going*, Presented at 4th International Intervisitation Program in Educational Administration, Vancouver

Culbertson, J. (1983) Theory in educational administration: echoes from critical thinkers, *Educational Researcher*, Vol. 12, No. 10, pp 15–22

Cuthbert R. (1984) *The Management Process*, E324 Management in Post Compulsory Education, Block 3, Part 2, Open University Press, Milton Keynes

Cyert, R.M. (1975) *The Management of Non Profit Organisations*, Lexington Books, Lexington, Massachusetts

Glatter, R. (1972) *Management Development for the Education Profession*, Harrap, London, for the University of London Institute of Education

Glatter, R. (1979) Educational policy and management: one field or two?, *Educational Analysis*, Vol. 1, No. 2, pp 15–24

Glatter, R. (1984) *Managing for Change*, E324 Management in Post Compulsory Education, Block 6, The Open University Press, Milton Keynes

Gray, H.L. (1979) *The School as an Organisation*, Nafferton Books, Nafferton

Greenfield, T.B. (1973) Organisations as social inventions: rethinking assumptions about change, *Journal of Applied Behavioural Science*, Vol. 9, No. 5, pp 551–574

Haag, D. (1982) *The Right to Education: What Kind of Management?*, Unesco, Paris

Handy, C. (1984) *Taken for Granted? Looking at Schools as Organisations*, Longman, York, for the Schools Council

Harries-Jenkins, G. (1984) State of the art review of the literature: education management, part 1, *School Organisation and Management Abstracts*, Vol. 3, No. 4, pp 213–233

Hoyle, E. (1981) *The Process of Management*, E323 Management and the School, Block 3, Part 1, Open University Press, Milton Keynes

Hughes, M.G. (1976) The professional as administrator: the case of the secondary school head. In R.S. Peters (Ed.) *The Role of the Head*, Routledge and Kegan Paul, London

Hughes, M.G. (1984) Educational administration: pure or applied, *Studies in Educational Administration*, Vol. 35, pp 1–10

Hughes, M.G., Carter, J. and Fidler, B. (1981) *Professional Development Provision for Senior Staff in Schools and Colleges*, University of Birmingham, Birmingham

Poster, C. (1976) *School Decision Making*, Heinemann, London

Taylor, W. (1976) The head as manager: some criticisms. In R.S. Peters (Ed.) *The Role of the Head*, Routledge and Kegan Paul, London

Walker, W.G. (1984) Administrative narcissism and the tyranny of isolation: its decline and fall 1954–1984, *Educational Administration Quarterly*, Vol. 20, No. 4, pp 6–23. Copyright © 1984 by W.G. Walker. Reprinted by permission of Sage Publications, Inc.

CHAPTER 2

MODELS OF EDUCATIONAL MANAGEMENT

The relevance of theory to good practice

Management is often regarded as essentially a practical activity. The determination of aims, the allocation of resources and the evaluation of effectiveness all involve action. Practitioners tend to be dismissive of theories and concepts for their alleged remoteness from the 'real' school situation. Dearden (1984, p. 4) claims that school and college staff have a somewhat ambivalent attitude towards theory:

> The teachers themselves commonly regard theory with a varying mixture of respect and suspicion: respect because it is thought of as difficult, and suspicion because its bearings are unclear on the detailed decision as to what to do next Monday morning.

There is some evidence that the explicit and systematic use of theory as a guide to practice is unusual. As Harries-Jenkins (1984) suggests, 'we are a long way from a unified view of theory and practice'. As a result there is a feeling that management is atheoretical. Willower (1980, p. 2), for example, asserts:

> [. . .] the application of theories by practising administrators [is] a difficult and problematic undertaking. Indeed, it is clear that theories are simply not used very much in the realm of practice.

Management decision-making is not a purely arbitrary activity. When a teacher or a manager takes a decision it reflects in part that person's view of the organization. Such views or preconceptions are coloured by experience and by the attitudes engendered by that experience. These attitudes take on the character of frames of reference or theories which necessarily influence the decision-making process. The manager may not be aware of the significance of theory which is often implicit rather than explicit.

The use of the term theory need not imply something remote from the day-to-day experience of the teacher. Rather theories and concepts can provide a framework for managerial decisions. As Landers and Myers (1977, p. 365) proclaim:

> [. . .] there is nothing more practical than a good theory. [. . .] It can [. . .] help the practitioner to unify and focus his views on an organisation, on his role and relationships within the organisation, and on the elusive phenomena of leadership and achievement.

It is suggested then that there is no real dichotomy between theory and practice. Rather theory serves to provide a rationale for decision-making. Managerial activity is enhanced by an explicit awareness of the theoretical framework underpinning practice in educational institutions. As a result some academics and practitioners 'now vigorously challenge the traditional view that practical on the job experience *on its own* provides adequate management training in education' (Hughes, 1984). There are three arguments to support the view that managers have much to learn from an appreciation of theory.

1. Reliance on facts as the sole guide to action is unsatisfactory because all evidence requires *interpretation*. Life in schools and colleges is too complex to enable practitioners to make decisions simply on an event by event basis. A frame of reference is needed to provide the insight for this important management task. As Bolman and Deal (1984) suggest, 'we have to develop patterns and frames in order to make sense of the complexities of everyday life'.
2. Dependence on *experience* in interpreting facts and making decisions is narrow because it discards the knowledge of others. Familiarity with the arguments and insights of theorists enables the practitioner to deploy a range of experience and understanding in resolving the problems of today. Walker (1984, p. 18) makes a convincing case for practitioner awareness of theory.

> As a result of the new horizons that have been opened up, scholars and practitioners alike have a much richer platform of ideas on which to base their diagnosis and to take action. A well prepared administrator can hardly avoid knowing that there is available to him or her a wide and challenging literature that promises useful alternatives for action.

3. Experience may be particularly unhelpful as the sole guide to action when the practitioner begins to operate in a different *context*. Organizational variables may mean that practice in one school or college has little relevance in the new environment. A broader awareness of theory may be valuable as the manager attempts to interpret behaviour in the fresh situation.

Of course theory is useful only so long as it has relevance to practice in education. The practitioner and the scholar have different purposes in gaining an appreciation of theory, as Theodossin (1982) makes clear: 'The academic tends to want understanding for knowledge, while the manager seeks understanding for action: to enable him to perceive the possible options open to him and the likely consequences of each.' This suggests that the relevance of theory for the manager in education may be judged by its value in assisting the resolution of practical problems inside schools and colleges.

The nature of theory in educational management

There is no single all-embracing theory of educational management. In part this reflects the astonishing diversity of educational institutions, ranging from small primary schools to huge universities and polytechnics. It relates also to the varied nature of the problems encountered in schools and colleges which require different approaches and solutions. Above all it reflects the nature of theory in education and the social sciences. House (1981) argues that theories or 'perspectives' in education are not the same as scientific theories. The latter comprise a set of beliefs, values and techniques that are shared within a particular field of enquiry. The dominant theory eventually comes under challenge by the emergence of new facts which the theory cannot explain. Subsequently a new theory is postulated which does explain these new facts. However, the physical world itself remains constant.

Theories of education and the social sciences are very different from scientific theories. These perspectives relate to a changing situation and comprise different ways of seeing a problem rather than a scientific consensus as to what is true. House suggests that, in this sense, the perspective is a weaker claim to knowledge than a scientific theory. In education several perspectives may be valid simultaneously while a scientific theory is closely defined by consensus of the relevant scientific community:

Our understanding of knowledge utilization processes is conceived not so much as a set of facts, findings, or generalisations but rather as distinct perspectives which combine facts, values and presuppositions into a complex screen through which knowledge utilisation is seen. [. . .] Through a particular screen one sees certain events, but one may see different scenes through a different screen. (House, 1981, p. 17)

The models discussed in this book should be regarded as alternative ways of portraying events, as House suggests, rather than the absolute truths of scientific theory. In choosing one perspective the teacher tends to exclude the other ways of understanding events. As Silverman (1970) suggests, 'all perspectives offer insights in exchange for limitations in approach'.

The perspectives favoured by managers are significant in that they inevitably influence or determine decision-making. Bolman and Deal (1984, p. 4) argue that perspectives or 'frames' form the basis for managerial practice:

Frames are windows on the world. Frames filter out some things while allowing others to pass through easily. Frames help us to order the world and decide what action to take.

Most theories of educational management possess three major characteristics:

1. Theories tend to be *normative* in that they reflect beliefs about the nature of educational institutions and the behaviour of individuals within them. To a greater or lesser extent theorists express views about how schools and colleges should be managed rather than simply describing aspects of the institution or explaining the organizational structure of the school or college. When, for example, practitioners or academics claim that decisions in schools are reached following a participative process they may be expressing normative judgements rather than analyzing actual practice.

2. Theories tend to be *selective* in that they emphasize certain aspects of the institution at the expense of other elements. The espousal of one theoretical model leads to the neglect of other approaches. Schools and colleges are arguably too complex to be capable of analysis through a single dimension. An explanation of educational institutions using a political perspective, for example, may focus on the formation of interest groups and on the bargaining between groups and individuals. This approach offers valuable insights as we shall see in Chapter 5. Yet this emphasis necessarily means that other valid characterizations of schools

and colleges are under represented. A few writers (Davies and Morgan, 1983; Ellstrom, 1983; Enderud, 1980) have presented syntheses of different approaches in an attempt to achieve an overall approach to organizations but with only limited success. This may be because theory development is at an early stage in educational management or because the differences between the various perspectives are too great to permit integration.

3. Theories of educational management are often based on, or supported by, *observation* of practice in educational institutions. The approaches developed initially for industrial or commercial organizations have been adapted, with varying success, for application to schools and colleges. Walker (1978, p. 100) asserts that theories require the support of regular and methodical observation.

> A crucial aspect of good theory development [. . .] relates to the area of systematic and repeated observation. Thus while it is possible to explain or predict a behaviour on the evidence of a single observation the prediction is very much more powerful if it is systematically and repeatedly observed.

While many theories of educational management are based on observation the subjective model is sceptical of this stance. As we shall see in Chapter 6 subjective theorists prefer to emphasize the perceptions and interpretations of individuals within organizations. In this view observation is suspect because it does not reveal the meanings placed on events by participants.

Those perspectives which are based on data from systematic observation are sometimes called 'grounded theory'. Because such approaches are derived from the educational context they are more likely to be perceived as relevant by practitioners in the schools and colleges. As Glaser and Strauss (1967) aptly claim, 'generating grounded theory is a way of arriving at theory suited to its supposed uses'.

Theory in educational management thus tends to be normative, selective and often based on observation in educational settings. These qualities overlap and interpenetrate as Theodossin (1983, p.89) demonstrates:

> Inevitably [. . .] research involves selection; selection is determined by, and determines, perspective; perspective limits vision; vision generates questions; and questions in turn, help to shape and influence the answers.

Models of educational management – an introduction

A substantial number of ideas or theories have been discussed by many different writers on educational management. These perspectives overlap along several different dimensions. A further complication is that similar models are given different names or, in certain cases, the same term is used to denote different approaches. Some aggregation of all these theories is needed so that they can be presented in a clear and discrete manner. Cuthbert (1984, p. 39) explains why there is a lack of clarity.

> The study of management in education is an eclectic pursuit. Models have been borrowed from a wide range of disciplines, and in a few cases developed specifically to explain unique features of educational institutions. To comprehend the variety of models available we need some labels and categories that allow us to consider different ideas in a sensible order.

Several writers have chosen to present theories in distinct groups or bundles but they differ both in the emphasis given to particular approaches and the terminology used to denote them. Bolman and Deal (1984) discuss three 'common sense perspectives' in seeking to analyze the nature of organizations. They choose to highlight the personalistic, rational and power perspectives. Theodossin (1982) explains educational institutions in terms of four perspectives – the environment, organizational structure, group interaction and the individual. Ellstrom (1983) suggests four organizational models as ways of characterizing schools and colleges – rational, political, social system and anarchistic. Cuthbert (1984) presents five models in seeking to describe the management of further and higher education. He emphasizes analytical-rational, pragmatic-rational, political, ambiguity and phenomenological models. Sergiovanni (1984) discusses four perspectives based on efficiency, the person, politics and the cultural view.

In this book the main theories and approaches are classified into five major models of educational management. This particular division is considered to be the most appropriate for a discussion of the wide range of British educational institutions. The five perspectives will be illustrated by examples of practice drawn from primary schools, secondary schools and colleges.

The models vary in the extent of their applicability to the different types of institution and, to a lesser degree, *within* any one sector of education. The five models are as follows:

1. Formal
2. Democratic
3. Political
4. Subjective
5. Ambiguity

The analysis of the five models includes consideration of four main elements which are valuable in distinguishing the different emphases of the models. The criteria are as follows:

1. The level of agreement within the staff about the *goals* or objectives of the institution. Analysts differ in that some emphasize organizational aims while others focus on individual purposes. Certain approaches feature agreement about objectives but others stress conflict over aims or point to difficulties in defining purpose within educational organizations.
2. The meaning and validity of organizational *structures* within educational institutions. According to some theorists structure is an objective fact while others believe that it is the subjective creation of individuals within the institution. A further group argue that structure is a matter for negotiation or dispute and other writers suggest that structure is one of the many ambiguous features of schools and colleges.
3. The relationship between the institution and its *environment*. Schools and colleges have to deal with a wide range of official and unofficial groups and with a host of individuals. The nature of these relationships is a key element in the differences between models. 'Any theory of organisations must specify the nature of their relationships with the wider society' (Silverman, 1970). Some writers treat schools and colleges as part of a 'system' of education while others stress the primacy of the institution in regulating links with external bodies. The conduct of these relationships is treated in a number of different ways by theorists. Some regard the head or principal as the sole or major contact with the outside world while others suggest a wider range of contacts. Links may be regarded as essentially cooperative in nature or they may be thought of as political, with conflict between the institution and external agencies. Other approaches emphasize the ambiguity of such relationships.
4. The most appropriate *leadership* strategies for educational institutions. Analysts have different views about the nature of educational leadership according to the theories they espouse. Some assume that heads take the lead in establishing objectives and in decision-making while others

regard the head as one figure within a participative system. Certain approaches stress conflict inside institutions and emphasize the head's role as negotiator while others point to the limitations of an active leadership role within essentially ambiguous institutions.

These criteria serve to emphasize the great differences in approach between the various models and reinforce the view that theories are normative and selective. Mangham (1979, pp. x–xi) argues that:

> [. . .] each of us approaches events and circumstances with bundles of values and related assumptions which constitute our basic frames of reference or conceptual models in terms of which we analyse and comment upon that with which we find ourselves confronted. Like it or not we do not see a *real* world that is truly there; each of us *interprets* his environment and copes with it by fitting it into meaningful patterns.

In the rest of this book we examine these different interpretations of the nature of organization and management in schools and colleges.

References

Bolman, L.G. and Deal, T.E. (1984) *Modern Approaches to Understanding and Managing Organisations*, Jossey Bass, San Francisco

Cuthbert, R. (1984) *The Management Process*, E324 Management in Post Compulsory Education, Block 3, Part 2, Open University Press, Milton Keynes

Davies, J.L. and Morgan, A.W. (1983) Management of higher education in a period of contraction and uncertainty. In O. Boyd-Barrett, T. Bush, J. Goodey, I. McNay and M. Preedy (Eds.) *Approaches to Post School Management*, Harper and Row, London

Dearden, R.F. (1984) *Theory and Practice in Education*, Routledge and Kegan Paul, London

Ellstrom, P.E. (1983) Four faces of educational organisations, *Higher Education*, Vol. 12, pp 231–241

Enderud, H. (1980) Administrative leadership in organised anarchies, *International Journal of Institutional Management in Higher Education*, Vol. 4, No. 3, pp 235–253

Glaser, B.G. and Strauss, A.L. (1967) *The Discovery of Grounded Theory*, Weidenfeld and Nicolson, London

Harries-Jenkins, G. (1984) State of the art review of the literature: education management, part 1, *School Organisation and Management Abstracts*, Vol. 3, No. 4, pp 213–233

House, E.R. (1981) Three perspectives on innovation. In R. Lehming and M. Kane (Eds.) *Improving Schools: using what we know*, Sage Publications, Beverly Hills

Hughes, M.G. (1984) Educational administration; pure or applied, *Studies in Educational Administration*, Vol. 35, pp 1–10

Landers, T.J. and Myers, J.G. (1977) *Essentials of School Management*, W.B. Saunders, Philadelphia

Mangham, I. (1979) *The Politics of Organisational Change*, Associated Business Press, Ludgate House, Fleet Street, London

Sergiovanni, T.J. (1984) Cultural and competing perspectives in administrative theory and practice. In T.J. Sergiovanni and J.E. Corbally, *Leadership and Organisational Culture*, University of Illinois Press, Chicago

Silverman, D. (1970) *The Theory of Organisations*, Gower, Aldershot

Theodossin, E. (1982) Managing education and management theory, *Coombe Lodge Reports*, Vol. 15, No. 4, pp 137–148

Theodossin, E. (1983) Theoretical perspectives on the management of planned educational change, *British Educational Research Journal*, Vol. 9, No. 1, pp 81–90

Walker, W.G. (1978) Values, unorthodoxy and the 'unscientific' in educational administration research, *Educational Administration*, Vol. 6, No. 2, pp 94–106

Walker, W.G. (1984) Administrative narcissism and the tyranny of isolation: its decline and fall, 1954–1984, *Educational Administration Quarterly*, Vol. 20, No. 4, pp 6–23. Copyright © 1984 W.G. Walker. Reprinted by permission of Sage Publications, Inc.

Willower, D.J. (1980) Contemporary issues in theory in educational administration, *Educational Administration Quarterly*, Vol. 16, No. 3 pp 1–25. Copyright © 1980 D.J. Willower. Reprinted by permission of Sage Publications, Inc.

"The approach to theory adopted in this book has certain similarities with Cuthbert's (1984) presentation of models in five distinct groups. Cuthbert's categories are analytic-rational, pragmatic-rational, political, models that stress ambiguity, and phenomenological and interactionist models. The latter three groups are the same as three of the models identified below although I prefer the term subjective rather than phenomenological or interactionist. Cuthbert compares his models in the following terms:

a) the level of agreement among people in the organization about the objectives of their joint efforts;
b) different ideas about the way in which performance can and should be evaluated;
c) different ideas about the concept and the meaning of organizational structure.

Two of the criteria used by Cuthbert are similar to two of the four criteria used below to distinguish different emphasis of the models."

CHAPTER 3

FORMAL MODELS

Central features of formal models

Formal model is an umbrella term used to embrace a number of similar but not identical approaches. These theories emphasize the official and structural elements of organizations. There is a focus on pursuing institutional objectives through rational approaches. The definition suggested below incorporates the main features of these perspectives:

> Formal models assume that organizations are hierarchical systems in which managers use rational means to pursue agreed goals. Heads possess authority legitimized by their formal positions within the organization and are accountable to sponsoring bodies for the activities of their institutions.

The various formal models have several common features:

1. They tend to treat organizations as *systems*. According to Moran (1972), 'a system [. . .] consists of a set of interacting parts and exhibits some kind of integrity as a whole'. This emphasis on interdependence implies that subunits such as departments or pastoral units are systemically related to each other and to the institution itself.
2. Formal models give prominence to the official *structure* of the organization. Formal structures are often represented by organization charts which show the authorized pattern of relationships between members of the institution. Structural models do not adequately reflect the many informal contacts within schools and colleges but they do help to represent the more stable and formal aspects of organizations.
3. In formal models the official structures of the organization tend to be

hierarchical. Organization charts emphasize vertical relationships between staff. In educational institutions staff are responsible to heads of department who, in turn, are answerable to heads and principals for the activities of their departments. The hierarchy thus represents a means of control for leaders over their staff. Renshaw (1974) asserts that 'most schools remain static, hierarchical and paternalistic in character. Internally they retain a tight authority structure.'

4. All formal approaches typify schools and colleges as *goal-seeking* organizations. The institution is thought to have official purposes which are accepted and pursued by members of the organization. Livingstone (1974), for example, claims that organizations and objectives are inevitably intertwined: 'Every organisation [. . .] has a goal towards which it strives [. . .] Having a purpose is inherent in the notion of organisation.' As hierarchical organizations it is assumed that heads and principals take the leading role in determining the goals of their institutions. 'Successful heads are *goal-orientated* insofar as they have a vision of how they would like to see their schools develop' (Coulson, 1985).

5. Formal models assume that managerial decisions are made through a *rational* process. Typically, all the options are considered and evaluated in terms of the goals of the organization. The most suitable alternative is then selected to enable those objectives to be attained. The essence of this approach is that decision-making is thought to be an objective, detached and intellectual process. Proponents of the rational model 'see the managerial elite as using rational and logical means to pursue clear and discrete ends set forth in official statements of goals' (Perrow, 1961).

6. Formal approaches present the *authority* of leaders as essentially a product of their official positions within the organization. Heads and principals possess authority over other staff because of their formal roles within schools and colleges. According to Ferguson (1980), these leaders exercise legitimate authority 'by virtue of office held at a particular time'.

7. In formal models there is an emphasis on the *accountability* of the organization to its sponsoring body. Educational institutions, then, are held to be responsible to the local education authority. Within hierarchies heads and principals in particular are answerable to the director of education for the activities of their organizations. As John (1980) suggests, 'a head is accountable for every aspect of the life of the school'. This necessarily includes the work of subordinates as well as their own performance.

The seven basic features are present to a greater or lesser degree in each of the individual theories which together comprise the formal models.

Structural models

The various approaches within the broad framework of formal models overlap significantly, along a number of dimensions. The main elements of each of these theories are often similar despite their different titles. There are variations in emphasis but the substantive components appear in most of the individual theories.

Structural models stress the primacy of organizational structure but the key elements are compatible with the central features of any formal model. Consider this passage from Bolman and Deal (1984, pp. 31–32):

> The structural perspective is based on a set of core assumptions:
>
> 1. Organizations exist primarily to accomplish established goals.
> 2. For any organization, there is a structure appropriate to the goals, the environment, the technology, and the participants.
> 3. Organizations work most effectively when environmental turbulence and the personal preferences of participants are constrained by norms of rationality.
> 4. Specialization permits higher levels of individual expertise and performance.
> 5. Coordination and control are accomplished best through the exercise of authority and impersonal rules.
> 6. Structures can be systematically designed and implemented.
> 7. Organizational problems usually reflect an inappropriate structure and can be resolved through redesign and reorganization.
>
> Structuralists tend to see organizations as relatively closed systems pursuing fairly explicit goals. Under those conditions, organizations can operate rationally with high degrees of certainty and predictability. If organizations are highly dependent on the environment, they are continually vulnerable to environmental influence or interference. To reduce their vulnerability, a variety of structural mechanisms are created to protect central activities from fluctuation and uncertainty.

The structural assumptions identified by Bolman and Deal, including the goal orientation, the rationality, the exercise of authority and the reference to systems, are in line with the central features of formal models discussed earlier. The structural categorization of organizations as relatively closed systems is not shared by some of the other approaches. Some theorists regard educational institutions as 'open systems'. However, the ability of schools and colleges to respond to their environments may depend on the responsiveness of their organizational structure (Clark, 1983).

Becher and Kogan (1980, p. 11) discuss a structural model which links the institution to the formal elements of its environment. The authors postulate four levels within the education system – central authorities, the institution, the 'basic unit' and the individual. The central level includes 'the various national and local authorities who are between them charged with overall planning, resource allocation and the monitoring of standards'. Basic units correspond with departments or faculties in colleges and with departments and pastoral groupings in schools.

This structural model features normative and operational modes:

> The first of these relates to the monitoring and maintenance of values within the system as a whole [. . .] The second, in contrast, refers to the business of carrying out practical tasks at different levels within the system. (Becher and Kogan, 1980, p. 13)

Relationships between levels can be categorized as either normative or operational. Normative relationships involve appraisal or judgement while operational relationships relate to the allocation of resources, responsibilities and tasks.

Becher and Kogan regard the links between the normative and operational modes as representing a state of dynamic equilibrium. Change is likely if the normative and operational elements at any level become significantly out of phase. Yet change may be difficult to accommodate unless it fits the existing structures of the institution. Curriculum innovation, for example, is unlikely unless it is sponsored by one of the existing basic units, or departments, and supported by the individuals within it. Becher and Kogan (1980) claim that 'many changes, including those generated from within, fail because they are unable to accommodate to existing structural constraints'.

It is significant that Becher and Kogan leave open the nature of the relationships between their four levels. As Figure 3.1 demonstrates, their structural model does not assume hierarchical relationships. The links between the four levels are presented as horizontal. In contrast school and college structures are usually portrayed as vertical and often specifically described as hierarchical. The structure of 'Sageton' comprehensive school, for example, is explicitly regarded as an authority structure (see Figure 3.2). 'The overall impression [. . .] is of an organisational structure which is both well defined and somewhat hierarchical and specialised' (Evans, 1983).

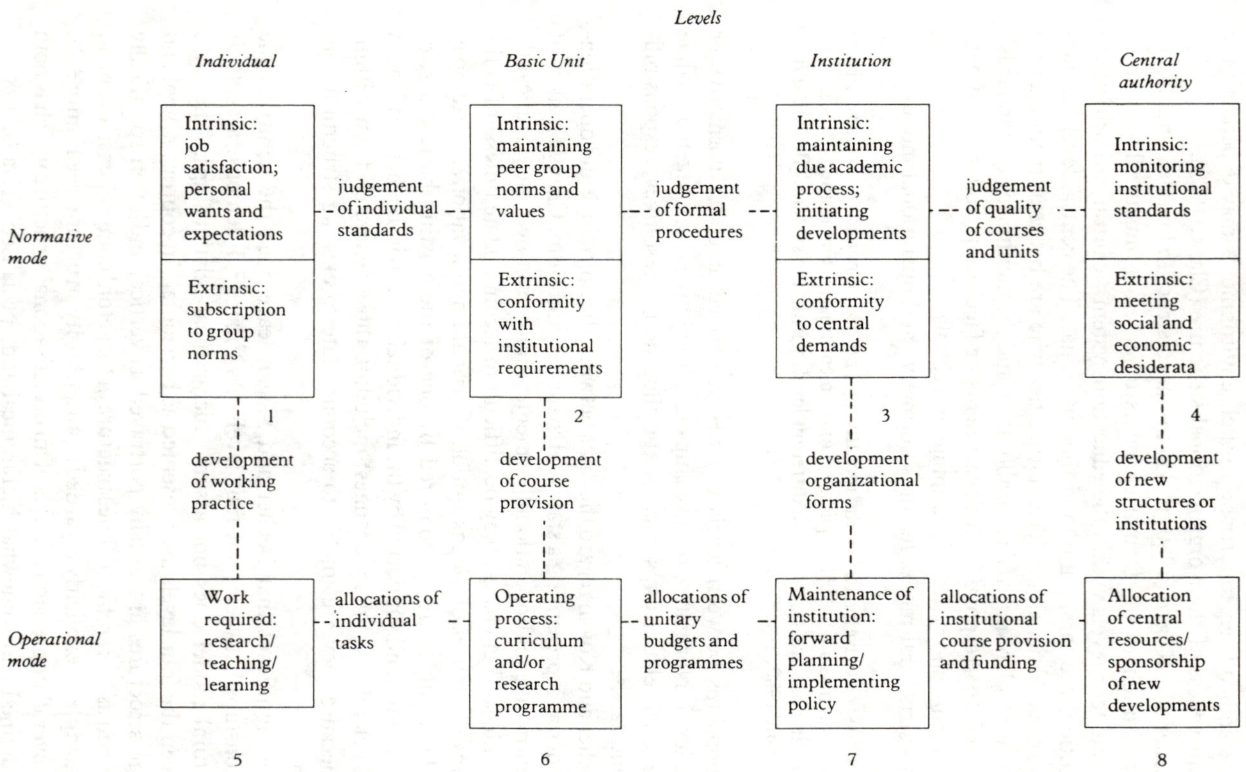

Levels

	Individual	*Basic Unit*	*Institution*	*Central authority*
Normative mode	Intrinsic: job satisfaction; personal wants and expectations Extrinsic: subscription to group norms	Intrinsic: maintaining peer group norms and values Extrinsic: conformity with institutional requirements	Intrinsic: maintaining due academic process; initiating developments Extrinsic: conformity to central demands	Intrinsic: monitoring institutional standards Extrinsic: meeting social and economic desiderata
Operational mode	Work required: research/teaching/learning	Operating process: curriculum and/or research programme	Maintenance of institution: forward planning/implementing policy	Allocation of central resources/sponsorship of new developments

Normative mode links:
- 1 — development of working practice / judgement of individual standards
- 2 — development of course provision / judgement of formal procedures
- 3 — development organizational forms / judgement of quality of courses and units
- 4 — development of new structures or institutions

Operational mode links:
- 5 — allocations of individual tasks
- 6 — allocations of unitary budgets and programmes
- 7 — allocations of institutional course provision and funding
- 8

Figure 3.1 A structural model (from Becher and Kogan, 1980)

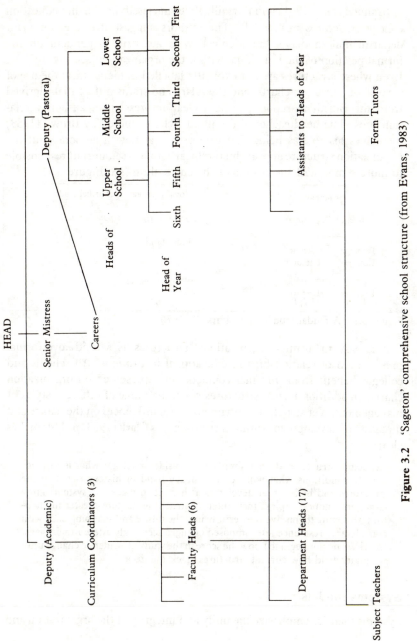

Figure 3.2 'Sageton' comprehensive school structure (from Evans, 1983)

Brannen *et al.* (1981) join Pursaill (1976) in classifying further education college structures as 'feudal'. The authors suggest that the dominant departmental model is 'hierarchical' with authority dependent on the formal position of the individual within the organization (see Figure 3.3). Even where structures are not explicitly labelled as hierarchical the use of vertical organization charts, and the salary and status differentials derived from the Burnham reports, gives a clear impression of authority relationships. The headteacher of the junior school studied by Brown (1983) 'perceives his role as being that of a democrat not an autocrat' but the organization structure appears hierarchical with less senior staff responsible to more senior staff for aspects of the curriculum (see Figure 3.4).

Principal	—	Royal prerogative or tribal leader
Head of Department	—	Baronial rights or *paterfamilias*
Principal Lecturer Senior Lecturer	—	Elder brothers
Lecturer I & II Lecturer I & II	—	Yeomen and serfs

Figure 3.3   A feudal model (from Pursaill, 1976)

It is easy to dismiss organizational structures as a rigid, overformal presentation of relationships in educational institutions. All schools and colleges benefit from informal contacts not represented on organization charts. In addition formal structures conceal a range of different styles of management. Yet structures remain powerful influences on the nature and direction of development within institutions, as Clark (1983, p. 114) makes clear:

> Academic structures do not simply move aside or let go: what is in place heavily conditions what will be. The heavy hand of history is felt in the structures and beliefs that development has set in place. As systems grow larger and more complex, their internal structures acquire greater momentum, thrusting themselves powerfully into the future and snapping back with considerable resilience after imposed changes seemingly altered their ways. [. . .] We do not begin to know the score in the study of academic change until we understand how current structures stack the deck.

Systems models

Systems theories emphasize the unity and integrity of the organization and

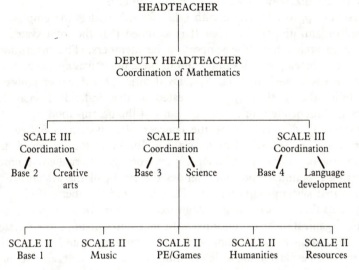

(close liaison between each 'Base' and 'Areas' of the curriculum')

Figure 3.4 Structure of a junior school (from Brown, 1983)

focus on the interaction between its component parts. Their advocates tend to be evangelical in pressing the merits of such models:

> Quality control and maximum effectiveness in a large educational organisation are possible only by use of the systems approach. This type of management is imperative in larger systems; it is also the key to producing better results in small school systems. (Landers and Myers, 1977, p. 416)

Systems models stress the unity and *coherence* of the organization. Schools and colleges are thought to have integrity as prime institutions. Members of the organization, and those external to it, recognize the school or college as a meaningful entity. Staff and students may feel that they 'belong' to the place where they teach or learn. There are dangers in too great an emphasis on the whole organization rather than the people within it, as Silverman (1970, p. 29) points out:

> Systems theorists believe that it is useful to follow the commonsense practice of attributing actions to organisations themselves as well as to the members of organisations [. . .] however, one runs the risk of attributing human characteristics to social constructs.

Greenfield (1973, 1975) has been the most persistent critic of this tendency to reify organizations as we shall see in Chapter 6.

Systems approaches share with other formal models the emphasis on agreed organizational *objectives*. It is assumed that the total system has objectives which have the support of its members. The institution is thought to develop policies in pursuit of these objectives and to assess the effectiveness of such policies. Systems theories play down or ignore the possibility that goals may be contested or that individuals may have purposes independent of the formal aims of the organization.

Systems models emphasize the concept of a system *boundary*. The boundary is an essential element in the definition of the system, distinguishing the organization and its members from the external environment. 'Drawing a boundary not only defines the extent of the system, it also defines that system's environment' (Latcham and Cuthbert, 1983).

Systems theories are usually categorized as either *closed* or *open* in terms of the organization's relationships with its environment. Closed systems tend to minimize transactions with the environment and to take little account of external opinion in determining the purposes and activities of the organization:

> Closed systems are static or deterministic in their relations with their environment and in the interaction of their component parts. Their boundaries are set and tend to resist penetration. (Landers and Myers, 1977, p. 398)

An example is the primary school practice of exhorting parents to leave their children at the school gates but this is much less common in the 1980s.

Open systems encourage interchanges with the environment, both responding to external influences and, in turn, seeking support for the objectives of the organization. In education, open systems theory shows the relationship between the institution and external groups such as parents, employers and the local education authority. Richman and Farmer (1974, p. 5) define open systems and point to their significance for the future of the institution.

> The organisation is viewed as transacting with external environmental elements with respect to the importing and exporting of money, people, energy, material, goods and services, information, and so on. [. . .] The exchange is an essential factor underlying the system's viability, its reproductive ability or continuity, and its ability to change.

Educational institutions vary considerably in the extent to which they may be regarded as closed or open systems. Further education colleges have extensive and vital links with employers, who sponsor students on many part-time and some full-time courses, and with validating bodies, who assess the suitability of course proposals. Community schools may also be regarded as open systems because of the constant interaction with various groups and individuals in the neighbourhood. Selective schools and certain universities, which enjoy high reputations and which do not have to compete vigorously for students, may be sufficiently impervious to external influences to be categorized as closed systems.

The distinction between open and closed systems is more blurred in practice than it is in theory. It may be more useful to think of a continuum rather than a sharp dichotomy between polarities. All schools and colleges have a measure of interaction with their environments but the greater the dependence of the institution on external groups the more 'open' it is likely to be. As parents increase their financial support so schools may be more open to influences over the ways in which money is spent and interaction is likely to increase in respect of several different aspects of school life.

Systems theorists believe that organizations can be categorized as systems with their parts interacting to achieve systemic objectives. However, caution should be exercised in attributing these qualities to educational institutions. Schools and colleges are complex human organizations and systems models may be inadequate, as Hoyle (1981, p. 12) emphasizes:

> Schools are certainly not organisations consisting of carefully articulated parts functioning harmoniously in the pursuit of agreed objectives. They are characterised by conflict, malintegration and the pursuit of individual and group interests. Nevertheless a certain degree of systematic integration is necessary for their effective functioning.

Bureaucratic models

The bureaucratic model is associated strongly with the work of Weber (1947). Weber argued that in formal organizations bureaucracy is the most efficient form of management. Some writers suggest that bureaucracy is an almost inevitable consequence of increasing size and complexity. Livingstone (1974, p. 9) argues that:

> bureaucracy describes only the simple truth that as organisations grow and become more complex, more formal systems of regulation replace the informal understanding that is often sufficient for effective co-ordination in the smaller, simpler units.

Bureaucracy, then, describes a formal organization which seeks maximum efficiency through rational approaches to management.

Bureaucratic models stress the importance of the *hierarchical authority structure* with formal chains of command between the different positions in the hierarchy. This pyramidal structure is based on the legal authority vested in the officers who hold places in the chain of command. Office holders are responsible to superiors for the satisfactory conduct of their duties. In educational institutions teachers are accountable to the head or principal in respect of their key teaching task.

In common with other formal models, bureaucratic approaches emphasize the *goal orientation* of the organization. Institutions are dedicated to goals which are clearly delineated by the officers at the apex of the pyramid. Ferguson (1980) claims that a bureaucracy 'has a common goal towards which members work under accepted leaders exercising legitimate authority'. Bureaucratic models assume that in schools and colleges goals are determined largely by the head or principal and endorsed without question by other staff.

Bureaucratic theories suggest a *division of labour* with staff specializing in particular tasks on the basis of expertise. The departmental structure in secondary schools and colleges is an obvious manifestation of division of labour with subject specialists teaching a defined area of the curriculum. In this respect primary schools do not resemble bureaucracies because staff are typically class teachers who work with one group of children for most or all aspects of the curriculum.

In bureaucracies decisions and behaviour are governed by *rules and regulations* rather than personal initiative. Harling (1984, p. 8) points to the advantages of a formal and impersonal set of rules:

> The regulations ensure a degree of uniformity of operation and together with the authority structure make possible the coordination of the various activities. Such regulations provide a degree of continuity regardless of changes in personnel, thus promoting stability.

Schools typically have rules to regulate the behaviour of pupils and often guide the behaviour of teachers through bureaucratic devices such as the staff handbook.

Bureaucratic models emphasize *impersonal* relationships between staff and clients. This neutrality is designed to minimize the impact of individuality on decision making. Good schools depend in part on the quality of personal relationships between teachers and pupils and this aspect of bureaucracy has little influence in many schools. Yet where schools require pupils to address staff as 'miss' or 'sir' they are promoting impersonal relationships and encouraging teachers to distance themselves from their students.

In bureaucracies the recruitment and career progress of staff are determined on *merit*. Appointments are made on the basis of qualifications and experience and promotion depends on expertise demonstrated in present and previous positions. Schools and colleges fulfil this criterion in that formal competitive procedures are laid down for the appointment of new staff and for some promoted posts. Internal promotions, however, depend on the recommendation of the head or principal and, in many cases, there is no formal process. A judgement about merit is unlikely to be completely impersonal when it is made by one individual and this aspect of career development in education does not fit the bureaucratic model.

All large organizations contain some bureaucratic elements and this is true of colleges and secondary schools. This perspective has certain advantages for education but there are difficulties in applying it too enthusiastically to institutions staffed by professionals:

> If professional expertise is concentrated near the base of the bureaucratic pyramid the rules themselves must be largely a product of the consent of those to whom they apply. If this consent is not forthcoming the organisation risks fragmenting into competitive interest groups. (Williams and Blackstone, 1983, p. 94)

Rational models

Rational approaches differ from other formal models in that they emphasize managerial *processes* rather than organizational structure or goals. The focus is on the process of decision-making instead of the structural framework which constrains but does not determine managerial decisions. This stress on process is the central element in Cuthbert's (1984, p. 39) definition of 'analytical-rational' models.

> Analytical-rational models are taken here to include all ideas of management as a process involving the rational and systematic analysis of situations, leading to identification and evaluation of possible courses of action, choice of a preferred alternative, implementation, and monitoring and review, in a cyclical and repetitive process. [. . .] The management process is depicted as a matter of systematic, informed, and rational decision-making.

Although the distinctive quality of rational models is their emphasis on process they share several characteristics with the other formal perspectives.

These include agreed organizational objectives and a bureaucratic organizational structure. The decision-making process thus takes place within a recognized structure and in pursuit of accepted goals. The process of rational decision-making is thought to have the following sequence:

1. Perception of a problem or a choice opportunity.
2. Analysis of the problem, including data collection.
3. Formulation of alternative solutions or choices.
4. Choice of the most appropriate solution to the problem to meet the objectives of the organization.
5. Implementation of the chosen alternative.
6. Monitoring and evaluation of the effectiveness of the chosen strategy.

The process is essentially iterative in that the evaluation may lead to a redefinition of the problem or a search for an alternative solution (see Figure 3.5).

Rational models have serious limitations as portrayals of the decision-making process in education. There may be dispute over objectives and the definition of problems is likely to be dependent on the particular standpoint of the individuals involved. In addition it may be that some of the data needed to make a decision is not available. Most problematic of all is the assumption that the choice of solution can be detached and impartial. In practice individuals and groups are likely to promote their own favoured

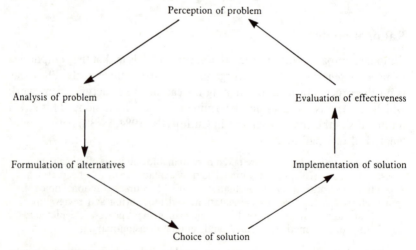

Figure 3.5 The rational process

solutions which in turn may reflect individual rather than organizational objectives. The perceived effectiveness of the chosen solution may also vary according to the predilections of the people concerned.

Despite the evident weaknesses of rational approaches they remain dominant in much of the literature on schools and colleges. In Chapter 2 we noted that theories tend to be *normative* in that they reflect views about how organizations and individuals ought to behave. Rational perspectives are the dominant normative models despite their practical limitations. Ellström (1983, p. 233) is right to claim that:

> in spite of the severe criticism that has been levelled against the rational model and its derivatives, its fundamental elements have, to a large extent, been retained as the predominant mode of organisational analysis.

Hierarchical models

Hierarchical approaches stress the vertical relationships within organizations and the accountability of leaders to external sponsors. The organizational structure is emphasized with particular reference to the authority and responsibility of the managers at the apex of the structure. Packwood (1977, p. 1) refers to the prevalence of the hierarchy in formal organizations and explains its significance:

> [. . .] the hierarchy is the general structure in all developed cultures for achieving work objectives that are beyond the control of the single individual. Through a series of manager–subordinate relationships it explicitly locates accountability for work. The manager in the hierarchy is accountable not only for his, or her, performance, but also for the work of subordinates.

In hierarchical models the organization structure is depicted as *pyramidal* with authority located at the top of the structure. Educational institutions are often typified in this way, as Lortie (1969, p. 4) suggests:

> The formal and legal allocation of authority in school systems is monolithic, hierarchical and concentrated; official powers are focused at the apex of the structure. A system of this kind implies that those in command set goals, oversee their realisation, and are accountable for outcomes.

Hierarchical approaches emphasize *vertical communication* patterns. Information is passed down the hierarchy to all appropriate levels and subordinates are expected to implement the decisions made by the senior managers. Difficult issues are referred upwards until they reach a level where they can be resolved. Horizontal communication plays little part in the hierarchy and such contacts as do occur are not part of the formal decision-making process. In schools and colleges the head or principal is thought to inform heads of department and other staff about policies and is the final arbiter of problems incapable of resolution at lower levels in the hierarchy.

Central to hierarchical models is the concept of *accountability*. Leaders are responsible to external agencies for the performance of subordinates and the activities of the organization. In schools the accountability of heads to the local education authority (LEA) and the governors is a major bulwark of their authority. Marriott (1981) claims that the junior school head has 'supreme legitimate authority' while Taylor (1983) asserts that 'ultimate responsibility for a school's performance resides with the head'.

Harling (1980) points to five areas where the primary head tends to have the decisive role:

(1) determination of the overall aims of the school;
(2) allocation of human and material resources;
(3) control of internal and external communications;
(4) formulation of school rules and regulations; and
(5) evaluation of staff and pupil progress.

The overarching role of primary school heads is modified in secondary schools and colleges where the sheer size mitigates against the personal involvement of heads and principals to the same extent. Nevertheless heads remain a powerful influence on the direction of any school because of their control over the system of rewards. As Hargreaves (1978) suggests, 'the teacher is very heavily dependent on the head – for allowances, for a "good" class, and for promotion. To get into the head's "bad books" is to risk career suicide.'

Hierarchical models have certain limitations when applied to educational institutions. Teachers as professionals claim discretion in their classroom work and there is a trend towards participation in decision-making on wider school issues. As a result 'the several strands of hierarchical control, collegial control, and autonomy become tangled and complex' (Lortie, 1969). Nevertheless the clear legal authority of the head suggests that hierarchical models cannot be dismissed as irrelevant for schools and colleges.

Formal models: goals, structure, environment and leadership

Formal models characterize schools and colleges as *goal oriented*. There is an assumption that institutions pursue specific objectives. These goals are invariably determined by heads and senior staff but formal approaches regard the support of other teachers as unproblematical. All members of the organization are thought to be working towards the achievement of these official aims. The activities and procedures of institutions are evaluated in terms of their relevance to the approved objectives, as Harling (1984, p. 7) suggests:

> The distinctive characteristic of an organisation is [. . .] that it has been formally established for the explicit purpose of achieving certain goals. Every organisation has a formally instituted pattern of authority and an official body of rules and procedures which are intended to aid the achievement of those goals.

The problem is that official goals are often so nebulous that they offer little guidance to action. At 'Jones' college, for example, Tipton (1973, p. 27) found that:

> because the official goals were vague there were plenty of grounds on which activities actually pursued, or mooted, could be justified if necessary; but equally, those who objected to certain activities stood a considerable chance of finding grounds on which to support their objections.

The portrayal of schools and colleges as organizations actively pursuing official goals set forth in formal statements is modified by certain writers who acknowledge the existence of multiple objectives in institutions. Beck and Cox (1984), for example, distinguish between personal goals, team goals and organizational goals. Similarly Livingstone (1974) differentiates between individual, departmental and formal goals. In a secondary school an official goal may refer to the fulfilment of the potential of all pupils. A departmental goal might relate to the attainment of particular standards of competence in certain subjects. Individual goals may well reflect personal career ambitions. Despite this recognition that goals may exist at different levels, there remains the clear implication that it is the official goals which guide the behaviour and decisions of staff. The possibility of conflict or ambiguity is often ignored or assumed away.

Formal models present organizational *structure* as an objective fact. Schools and colleges are 'real' institutions which induce a sense of belonging in teachers and pupils alike. They are thought to define their lives in terms of their position within the school or college. Structures may be typified in physical terms that imply permanence (see Figures 3.2, 3.3 and 3.4). Individuals are accorded a place in the structure such as teacher of class 2 or head of the physics department. These structural considerations are assumed to influence the behaviour of the individuals holding particular roles in the organization. Structure is regarded as established rather than the creation of individuals within the institution.

Formal approaches differ in the way they typify relationships between the organization and its *environment*. The more rigid models, such as 'closed systems' or structural theories, tend to limit environmental links to the minimum required to sustain accountability. These perspectives characterize relationships in terms of the official links between the head or principal and such formal groups as the LEA and the governing body. Interaction with other groups, such as parents, employers and educational institutions, is de-emphasized. 'Closed' models assume that schools or colleges are impervious to such influences.

Other formal models, such as 'open systems', postulate wide-ranging links with the environment. Educational institutions are portrayed as interactive organizations, responding to a changing environment and displaying their achievements to the local community. At a time of falling rolls, spending limitations and youth unemployment, schools and colleges are increasingly adopting a more 'open' stance, conscious of the need for a good reputation with parents, employers and the decision-makers at county hall. Few educational institutions justify the label 'closed' in the 1980s.

Within formal models *leadership* is ascribed to the person at the apex of the hierarchy. It is assumed that this individual sets the tone of the organization and establishes the major official objectives. Baldridge *et al.* (1978, p. 44) consider the nature of formal leadership:

> Under the bureaucratic model the leader is seen as the hero who stands at the top of a complex pyramid of power. The hero's job is to assess the problems, consider alternatives, and make rational choices. Much of the organisation's power is held by the hero, and great expectations are raised because people trust him to solve problems and fend off threats from the environment.

The leader is expected to play the key part in policy-making, and implementation of change is assumed to follow. The possibility of opposition, or indifference, to change is not acknowledged. It is believed that implementation is unproblematic:

> This is not to say that others, further down the hierarchy, will not require

information and explanation, nor that there will not be problems, but that the flow of information is down the hierarchy and is dependent upon acceptance of a policy, plan or decision at the top. (Hewton, 1982, p. 35)

In education several features tend to support this characteristic of unidimensional leadership. Official bodies and individuals behave as if the head or principal is the fount of all knowledge and authority. The Department of Education and science (DES) model articles of school management are unequivocal in stating that 'the headteacher shall control the internal organisation, management and discipline of the school'. The head is the focal point for most external communication and even the most junior clerk in the local education office expects to contact the school via the head. Many other groups tend to regard the head or principal as the public face of the institution and behave accordingly. Particularly in the primary school there is a perceived identity between the head and the school which reinforces the 'top down' leadership perspective. 'Because of his formal authority the head represents and symbolises the school both to people inside it and to members of the community' (Coulson, 1985).

The assumption of an all powerful leader at the apex of schools and colleges has several limitations. While formal authority resides with the head, power is inevitably shared with other professional staff. At a minimum heads require the consent of colleagues if policy initiatives are to be carried through into departmental and classroom practice. In certain circumstances their authority may be compromised by other power groups within and outside the institution. Governors, parents, unions and staff all seek to influence decisions and action and this tends to limit the effective authority of the head. Research by Taylor (1983, pp. 284–286) suggests that the formal position of heads as all powerful leaders is in contrast with the reality of a daily struggle to maintain their authority in the face of mounting pressures:

> The sense of a diminishing freedom to manage was the greatest concern of heads [. . .] The disjunction between the head's statutory responsibilities and his freedom to manage is surely no longer acceptable.

The validity of formal models is reduced by such evidence of conflict or ambiguity.

The limitations of formal models

The various formal models pervade much of the literature on educational management. They are normative approaches in that they present ideas about how people in organizations *ought* to behave. So schools and colleges are typified as goal-seeking organizations employing rational means to achieve the objectives established by official leaders. Yet for staff of educational institutions this framework seems inadequate. As one experienced secondary head suggests, 'there is the greatest discrepancy between the declared rational process and the undeclared, often unperceived, reality' (Marland, 1982).

Formal models are selective as well as normative. In focusing on the bureaucratic and structural aspects of organizations they necessarily ignore or underestimate other salient features. Griffiths (1978) claims that formal approaches 'have limited our view of what an organisation is and how it operates' while Hughes (1978) argues that bureaucratic models 'provide only a first approximation to an understanding of school organisation'.

There are five specific weaknesses associated with formal models:

1. It is unrealistic to characterize schools and colleges as *goal-oriented* organizations. It is often difficult to ascertain the goals of educational institutions. Few schools have formal written statements of their objectives such as exist, for example, in university charters. This difficulty may be overcome by assuming that public statements made by heads represent the purposes of the institution. However, these formal objectives may have little value, as Perrow (1961, p. 855) demonstrates:

> Official goals are purposely vague and general and do not indicate two major factors which influence organisational behaviour: the host of decisions that must be made among alternative ways of achieving official goals and the priority of multiple goals, and the many unofficial goals pursued by groups within the organisation. [. . . These] operative goals designate the ends sought through the actual operating policies of the organisation; they tell us what the organisation actually is trying to do, regardless of what the official goals say are the aims.

Even if it is possible to establish the purposes of schools and colleges there are further problems in judging whether objectives have been achieved. Many of the goals associated with education are very difficult to measure. How do you assess whether pupils have reached their potential? The relationship between purposes and actions is not as tidy as the protagonists of formal models proclaim. It is unrealistic to assume that decisions in schools necessarily reflect their defined objectives. Rather they result from the more immediate needs of the situation: 'Organisational decisions are rarely triggered by preconceived goals [. . .] but usually by situations which constitute a pressure to act' (Mayntz, 1976). Classroom incidents, for example, require rapid responses and there is often little opportunity to evaluate possible decisions against school goals before taking action.

2. The portrayal of decision-making as a *rational* process is fraught with difficulties. The belief that managerial action is preceded by a process of evaluation of alternatives and a considered choice of the most appropriate option is rarely substantiated. Decisions in schools and colleges are made by teachers, who draw on a whole range of experience and idiosyncracy as they respond to events. Much of human behaviour is irrational and this inevitably influences the nature of decision-making in education. Weick (1976, p. 1) asserts that rational practice is the exception rather than the norm:

> People in organisations, including educational organisations, find themselves hard pressed either to find actual instances of those rational practices or to find rationalised practices whose outcomes have been as beneficent as predicted, or to feel that those rational occasions explain much of what goes on within the organisation. Parts of some organisations are heavily rationalised but many parts also prove intractable to analysis through rational assumptions.

Educational institutions, in common with other organizations staffed by professionals, depend on decisions made at individual and small group levels. Professional judgement is based as much on the intuition and background of the individual as on rational processes conditioned by the rule book. Shaw (1983) points to the limits of rationality in education: 'Schools and colleges are relatively small, scattered, internally complex units, heavily responsive to their immediate local context: guerrilla warfare not guided missiles.'

3. Formal models focus on the organization as an entity and ignore or underestimate the contribution of *individuals* within organizations. Critics of formal perspectives, notably Greenfield (1973), allege that such approaches treat organizations as if they were independent of the people within them. Theorists are said to attribute human characteristics to organizations. This process of reification occurs with statements like 'the local primary is a good school' or 'the objective of this school is to achieve good results in public examinations'.

Greenfield's alternative approach to organizations is discussed in Chapter 6 but the essence of his argument is that organizations are the creation of the people within them. All formal models give primacy to the organization and individuals are subordinated to organizational requirements. Structural and hierarchical approaches focus on the organizational structure and assume that individuals occupy preordained positions in the structure. Their roles are defined in terms of their position in the structure. Staff are portrayed as head of English or teacher of class 3 rather than John Brown or Janet Green. It is assumed that their behaviour reflects their places in the organization rather than their individual qualities and experience. Critics of formal models argue that they greatly underestimate individual variables and thus produce an inaccurate picture of educational institutions. As Sayer graphically illustrates, many teachers feel that this is a gross misrepresentation of educational institutions:

> A school is not a unit; it may be a convenient fiction in a telephone directory or an administrator's inventory, but the only unit in education is a human being. (quoted in Poster, 1976, p. 88)

4. A central assumption of formal models is that power resides at the apex of the pyramid. Heads and principals possess authority by virtue of their position as the appointed leaders of the institution. This focus on official authority leads to a view of institutional management which is essentially *top down*. Policy is laid down by senior managers and implemented by staff lower down the hierarchy. Their acceptance of managerial decisions is regarded as unproblematic.

These hierarchical approaches are most relevant to organizations which depend on tight discipline for their effectiveness. The armed forces are expected to carry out their orders without any questioning or elaboration. The situation is assumed to require compliance with instructions from superordinates. In industrial and commercial settings there is also some emphasis on official power with policy and decision-making centred on senior management. Most early applications of management theory in education were derived from the business world to the evident discomfort of certain educationists. Taylor (1976, p. 41) regards the use of models derived from industry with suspicion:

> The business analogy is [. . .] seen by some as unfortunate in that it tends to encourage a 'them' and 'us' relationship between head, senior staff, teachers and students, instead of stressing shared values within an academic community.

Organizations with large numbers of professional staff tend to exhibit signs of tension between the conflicting demands of professionalism and the hierarchy. Formal models assume that leaders, because they are appointed on merit, have the competence to issue appropriate instructions to subordinates. This is supported by the authority vested in them by virtue of their official position. Professional organizations have a rather different ethos with expertise distributed widely within the organization. Where professionals specialize, as in secondary schools and colleges, the ability of leaders to direct the actions of subordinates may be questionable. A head who is a classics graduate lacks the competence to supervise teaching in the faculty of craft and design. Similarly a head of science who is a physicist may be unable to monitor the teaching of a biologist within the department. In professional organizations, then, there is an authority of expertise which may come into conflict with positional authority. Hughes (1978) discusses this paradox:

> [. . .] it is through the independent exercise of his trained judgement, irrespective of his formal position, that the expert makes his contribution to an organisation. It is through precisely the same activity that the expert comes into conflict with the administrative hierarchy. Furthermore, it is unsafe to assume under all circumstances that technical expertise necessarily, or even generally, increases with position in the formal hierarchy.

The presence of significant numbers of professionals in organizations leads to an uncertain relationship between the leader and other staff. The professional's authority of expertise jostles with the leader's formal authority as head of the organization with accountability to external bodies. Consider this passage from Hoyle (1981, p. 16):

> *Head*: I'm a little concerned Mr Dingle, that your English lessons pay little attention to inculcating good standards in written English.
> *Dingle*: I'm sorry to hear that, but I would like to know how you have come to your views on what goes on in my classes and, as a physicist, what knowledge you have in the teaching of English?
> *Head*: Mr Dingle, I regard those two questions as impertinent. I know what goes on in your classroom because I hear from other members of staff and from disgruntled parents who have been to complain. And although I am a physicist, I have been in this game long enough to know something about the teaching of English. In any case, as head of this school I am responsible for what goes on in it, and I don't like what I hear of your approach to the subject.
> *Dingle*: I'm sorry to hear that, headmaster, but as a professional I must insist on teaching English in the best way in which I know how.

This extract illustrates the problem facing heads. They are responsible for the quality of the teaching process in their school and yet their authority over teachers is uncertain in respect of professional matters. Professional staff claim zones of autonomy based on their specialist expertise. The classroom is the domain of the teacher and pedagogic matters are the responsibility of the practitioner as a qualified professional. These areas of discretion may lead to conflict with heads seeking to exert their authority. Ultimately such difficulties can be avoided only if there is at least tacit acceptance of the head's overall responsibility for the activities of the school. This involves the recognition by teachers of the head's right to take the initiative in many areas of school policy. In professional organizations, then, staff must accept the leader's authority if it is to be effective.

5. Formal approaches are based on the implicit assumption that organizations are relatively *stable*. Individuals may come and go but they slot into predetermined positions in a static structure. Bureaucratic and structural theories are most appropriate in stable conditions as Bolman and Deal (1984) suggest: 'The structural frame helps to capture the more stable and formal aspects of human behaviour in organisations.'

It can be argued that assumptions of stability are unrealistic in many organizations and invalid in most schools and colleges. March and Olsen (1976) are right to claim that 'individuals find themselves in a more complex, less stable and less understood world than that described by standard theories of organisational choice'. Rational perspectives require a measure of predictability to be useful as portraits of organizational behaviour. Yet educational institutions depend on interpersonal relationships which may be volatile. The validity of formal models may be reduced further during periods of rapid change. Heads in secondary schools studied by Taylor (1983, p. 277) refer to 'the sheer weight of externally imposed change' and one points to its effects:

> Long-term planning gives way to planning one or two years ahead at most, and often less. Constant battering, relentless change, means the need to adapt, respond, react to events, rather than measured actions.

In changing, dynamic, unstable organizations there may be little time or opportunity to engage in a rational process of choice. The idea of a thorough analysis of a problem followed by identification of alternatives, choice of the preferred option and a process of implementation and evaluation may be unrealistic in a period of rapid change. Rather the manager often has to make a quick decision based on inadequate data. In education it may well be true that 'the loss of the stable state attacks the social underpinnings of rational knowledge' (Schon, 1971).

These criticisms of formal models suggest that they have serious limitations in respect of schools and colleges. The significance of the hierarchy is compromised by the expertise possessed by professional staff. The official authority of leaders has to vie with the professional authority of the teachers. The alleged rationality of the decision-making process requires modification to allow for the pace of change and the nature of personal relationships in schools and colleges. The idea of organizational goals is challenged by those who point to the existence of multiple objectives in education and the possible conflict between goals held at individual, departmental and institutional levels. However, it would be inappropriate to dismiss formal approaches as irrelevant to schools and colleges. These theories remain valid as *partial* descriptions of organization and management in education. As Harling (1984) suggests, 'the purely formal models are inadequate but certainly not defunct'.

References

Baldridge, J. V., Curtis, D.V., Ecker, G. and Riley, G.L. (1978) *Policy-Making and Effective Leadership*, Jossey Bass, San Francisco

Becher, T. and Kogan, M. (1980) *Process and Structure in Higher Education*, Gower, Aldershot

Beck, J. and Cox, C. (1984) Developing organisational skills. In C. Cox and J. Beck (Eds.) *Management Development: Advances in Practice and Theory*, John Wiley, New York

Bolman, L.G. and Deal, T.E. (1984) *Modern Approaches to Understanding and Managing Organisations*, Jossey Bass, San Francisco

Brannen, R., Holloway, D. and Peeke, G. (1981) Departmental Organisational Structures in Further Education, *Journal of Further and Higher Education*, Vol. 5, No. 3, pp 22–32

Brown, C.M. (1983) Curriculum management in the junior school, *School Organisation*, Vol. 3, No. 3, pp 221–228

Clark, B.R. (1983) The contradictions of change in academic systems, *Higher Education*, Vol. 12, pp 101–116

Coulson, A. (1985) *The Managerial Behaviour of Primary School Heads*, Collected Original Resources in Education, Carfax Publishing Company, Abingdon

Cuthbert, R. (1984) *The Management Process*, E324 Management in Post Compulsory Education, Block 3, Part 2, The Open University Press, Milton Keynes

Ellström, P.E. (1983) Four faces of educational organisations, *Higher Education*, Vol, 12, pp 231–241

Evans, J. (1983) Decision-making, conflict and control in comprehensive schooling: the management or harassment of curriculum reform, *School Organisation*, Vol. 3, No. 4, pp 345–360

Ferguson, C. (1980) Alternative organisational structures in higher and further education, *Coombe Lodge Reports*, Vol. 12, No. 12, pp 535–572

Greenfield, T.B. (1973) Organisations as social inventions: rethinking assumptions about change, *Journal of Applied Behavioural Science*, Vol. 9, No. 5, pp 551–574

Greenfield, T.B. (1975) Theory about organisations: a new perspective and its implications for schools. In M. Hughes (Ed.) *Administering Education: International Challenge*, Athlone Press, London

Griffiths, D.E. (1978) Contemporary theory development and educational administration, *Educational Administration*, Vol. 6, No. 2, pp 80–93

Hargreaves, D. (1978) Do we need headteachers? In C. Richards (Ed.) *Education 3–13*, Nafferton Books, Nafferton

Harling, P. (1980) School decision-making and the primary headteacher, *Education 3–13*, Vol. 8, No. 2, pp 44–48

Harling, P. (1984) The organisational framework for educational leadership. In P. Harling (Ed.) *New Directions in Educational Leadership*, Falmer Press, Lewes

Hewton, E. (1982) *Rethinking Educational Change*. Society for Research into Higher Education, Guildford

Hoyle, E. (1981) *The Process of Management*, E323 Management and the School, Block 3, Part 1, Open University Press, Milton Keynes

Hughes, M.G. (1978) Reconciling professional and administrative concerns, Commonwealth Council for Educational Administration, *Studies in Educational Administration*, 13

John, D. (1980) *Leadership in Schools*, Heinemann, London

Landers, T.J. and Myers, J.G. (1977) *Essentials of School Management*, W.B. Saunders, Philadelphia

Latcham, J. and Cuthbert, R. (1983) A systems approach to college management. In O. Boyd-Barrett, T. Bush, J. Goodey, I. McNay and M. Preedy (Eds.) *Approaches to Post-School Management*, Harper and Row, London.

Livingstone, H. (1974) *The University: An Organisational Analysis*, Blackie, Glasgow

Lortie, D.C. (1969) The balance of control and autonomy in elementary school teaching. In A. Etzioni (Ed.) *The Semi-Professions and Their Organisation*, Free Press, a division of Macmillan, Inc., New York

March, J.G. and Olsen, J.P. (1976) Organisational choice under ambiguity. In J.G. March and J.P. Olsen, *Ambiguity and Choice in Organisations*, Universitetsforlaget, Bergen

Marland, M. (1982) The politics of improvement in schools, *Educational Management and Administration*, Vol. 10, No. 2, pp 119–134

Marriott, S. (1981) Patterns of authority and autonomy in three junior schools, *Durham and Newcastle Research Review*, Vol. 9, No. 47, pp 269–278

Mayntz, R. (1976) Conceptual models of organisational decision-making and their application to the policy process. In G. Hofstede and M.S. Kassen (Eds.) *European Contributions to Organisation Theory*, Van Gorcum, Assen

Moran, W.E. (1972) A systems view of university organisation. In P.W. Hamelman (Ed.) *Managing the University: A Systems Approach*, Praeger, New York

Packwood, T. (1977) The school as a hierarchy, *Educational Administration*, Vol. 5, No. 2, pp 1–6

Perrow, C. (1961) The analysis of goals in complex organisations, *American Sociological Review*, Vol. 26, pp 854–856

Poster, C. (1976) *School Decision-Making*, Heinemann, London

Pursaill, A.J. (1976) Staff development in FE at a time of crisis, *Coombe Lodge Reports* 9, pp 277–285

Renshaw, P. (1974) Education and the primary school – a contradiction? *Education for Teaching*, Vol. 93, pp 8–16

Richman, B.M. and Farmer, R.N. (1974) *Leadership, Goals and Power in Higher Education*, Jossey Bass, San Francisco

Schon, D.A. (1971) *Beyond the Stable State*, Temple Smith, London

Shaw, K.E. (1983) Rationality, experience and theory, *Educational Management and Administration*, Vol. 11, No. 3, pp 167–172

Silverman, D. (1970) *The Theory of Organisations*, Gower, Aldershot

Taylor, K. (1983) Heads and the freedom to manage, *School Organisation*, Vol. 3, No. 3, pp 273–286

Taylor, W. (1976) The head as manager: some criticisms. In R.S. Peters (Ed.) *The Role of the Head*, Routledge and Kegan Paul, London

Tipton, B.F.A. (1973) *Conflict and Change in a Technical College*, Hutchinson, London

Weber, M. (1947) In T. Parsons (Ed.) *The Theory of Social and Economic Organisation*, Free Press, Glencoe, Illinois and Collier-Macmillan, New York

Weick, K.E. (1976) Educational organisations as loosely coupled systems, *Administrative Science Quarterly*, Vol. 21, No. 1, pp 1–19

Williams, G. and Blackstone, T. (1983) *Response to Adversity*, Society for Research into Higher Education, Guildford

CHAPTER 4

DEMOCRATIC MODELS

Central features of democratic models

Democratic models include all those theories which emphasize that power and decision-making are shared among some or all members of the organization. These approaches range from a 'restricted' democracy where the leader shares power with a limited number of senior colleagues to a 'pure' democracy where all members have an equal voice in determining policy. The definition suggested below captures the main features of these perspectives:

> Democratic models assume that organizations determine policy and make decisions through a process of discussion leading to consensus. Power is shared among some or all members of the organization who are thought to have a mutual understanding about the objectives of the institution.

Democratic models have the following major features:

1. They are strongly *normative* in orientation. We have already noted that all theories tend to be normative but democratic approaches in particular reflect the prescriptive view that management ought to be based on agreement. Their advocates believe that decision-making should be based on democratic principles but do not necessarily claim that these principles actually determine the nature of management in action. Democratic models are founded on values and beliefs but may not be grounded in reality. 'It is a rather ambiguous concept that favours full participation in decision-making. It is a utopian prescription of how the educational process should operate' (Richman and Farmer, 1974).

2. Democratic approaches are perhaps particularly appropriate for organizations with significant numbers of professional staff. Professionals possess authority arising directly from their knowledge and skill. They have an *authority of expertise* in contrast to the official authority associated with formal models. Professional authority occurs where decisions are made on an individual basis rather than being standardized. Education necessarily demands a professional approach because pupils and students need personal attention. Teachers require a measure of autonomy in the conduct of their professional activities. Democratic models assume that staff also have a right to share in the wider decision-making process. As Noble and Pym (1970, p. 433) suggest:

> [. . .] the claim inherent in professionalism to self-determination in the exercise of professional functions was extended beyond the areas of strictly professional competence into the sphere of general organisational planning and its detailed execution. The extension of the dominant professional ethic to the administration of a large organisation implied the right of status equals to be respected and consulted.

3. Democratic models assume a *common set of values* held by members of the organization. These may arise from the socialization which occurs during training and the early years of professional practice. Teacher training and the probationary year are obvious examples of this process of socialization. These common values guide the managerial activities of the organization and in particular are thought to lead to shared institutional objectives. The common background and education of participants form part of the justification for the normative assumption that it is always possible to reach agreement about goals and policies. According to Richman and Farmer (1974, p. 29), the democratic model:

> has a very strong harmony bias that assumes away the possibility of conflict. It is only likely to work well [. . .] where virtually all of the participants – especially the more active ones – have a strong spirit of genuine co-operation, similar values and personal goals, and a deep commitment to the institution and its goals and priorities.

4. Most democratic theories build in the assumption that staff have *formal representation* within the various decision-making bodies. Significant areas of policy are determined within the official committee system rather than being the prerogative of individual leaders. The democratic element of formal representation rests on the allegiance owed by representatives to their constituencies. A teacher representing the English department on a committee is accountable to colleagues because they have the right to

nominate or elect another person if they are not happy about the way they are being represented.

Informal consultations with staff do not constitute a truly democratic approach. Where heads seek the advice of colleagues before making a decision the process is one of consultation whereas the essence of democracy is participation in decision-making. Power is shared with staff in a democracy rather than remaining the preserve of the leader. Formal representation confers the right to participate in defined areas of policy while informal consultation is at the sole discretion of the leader who is under no obligation to act on the advice received.

5. Democratic models assume that decisions are reached by a process of *consensus* or compromise rather than division or conflict. The belief that there are common values and shared objectives leads on to the view that it is both desirable and possible to resolve issues by agreement. This is not to say that there will be no differences of opinion but rather that they can be overcome by the force of argument. The decision-making process may be elongated by the search for compromise but this is regarded as an acceptable price to pay to maintain the aura of shared values and beliefs. This feature is probably at its strongest in higher education. Moodie and Eustace (1974, p. 221), for example, claim that:

> the ideal of rule by consensus underlines the important and widespread feeling that, at least with respect to major policy decisions, no simple majoritarian system can successfully be operated within a university. Instead the stress is placed upon discussion and persuasion as the proper means to securing agreement upon the most important decisions.

Democratic models in higher education

Democratic approaches in British education originated within the colleges of Oxford and Cambridge universities. The style of management developed there is known as the *collegial* model:

> Collegium designates a structure or structures in which members have equal authority to participate in decisions which are binding on each of them. It usually implies that individuals have discretion to perform their main operations in their own way, subject only to minimal collegial controls. (Becher and Kogan 1980, p. 67)

The collegial model has been adopted within most universities. The authority of expertise is widespread within these institutions of advanced learning and research. They are, in Glatter's (1984) terms 'bottom-heavy institutions' and the nature of management reflects this wide distribution of knowledge and competence. Williams and Blackstone (1983) claim that 'any organisation which depends on high-level professional skills operates most efficiently if there is a substantial measure of collegiality in its management procedures'.

The collegial model is most evident within the extensive committee system. Decisions on a whole range of academic and resource allocation issues take place within a labyrinth of committees rather than being the prerogative of the vice-chancellor. Issues are generally resolved by agreement or compromise rather than by voting or dissent. As Williams and Blackstone (1983) suggest, 'the members of a college take their own collective decisions, which have an authority legitimised by consensus, or at least compromise, amongst those to whom they apply'.

Collegial approaches fit within the democratic model but in many universities democracy is compromised by a limited franchise. Certain institutions give full voting rights to all academic staff and some representation to students and perhaps also non-academic staff. Elsewhere membership of senate and the key committees is the preserve of senior staff. Moodie and Eustace (1974, p. 223) regard these constituency variations as a significant defect for a democratic approach:

> The [. . .] main shortcoming of consensual democracy relates to the criteria by which citizenship should be defined. Among what precise group of more or less equal citizens should consensus be obtained in this kind of democratic system? Is there, in particular, any good reason for extending citizenship beyond the restricted group of equal [. . .] professors to all members of the academic staff.

The main justification for a restricted franchise relates to academic expertise. Perhaps only senior members of the university can claim that authority of expertise which is a central criterion of collegial models. However, a tight interpretation of expertise calls into question the suitability of a 'democratic' label for management models in universities. In some institutions an 'elite' theory would be more appropriate. 'Democracy is thus, in our view, a term which should be applied with much greater care than is customary in discussions of university government if, indeed, it should be applied at all' (Moodie and Eustace, 1974, p. 224).

Despite the limitations of university democracy the collegial model was adopted when changes were proposed for public sector colleges (DES, 1966). Most polytechnics and higher education colleges have introduced an academic board to parallel the university senate. Academic boards generally have a mixture of elected and *ex officio* members, which limits the democratic element of college management. The composition of the academic board at Cambridgeshire College of Arts and Technology is perhaps fairly typical:

> The academic board consists of the principal (chairman), the vice-principal, the eight heads of department, the chief administrative officer, the college librarian, the chairmen of the degree and general councils, three student members nominated by the students' union, and twelve members of the full time teaching staff (eight of whom are elected by departments and the remainder by the full time teaching staff as a whole). From 1982 there has been an elected non-teaching staff representative on the academic board. (Bush and Goulding, 1984, p. 17)

There is a dichotomy in colleges between academic policy which is generally the responsibility of the 'democratic' academic board and resource management which is usually the preserve of the principal and heads of department. The committee system fits the democratic model while the powers accorded directly to senior managers suggest one of the formal models. Kogan (1984, p. 28) points to the risk of conflict between the democratic and hierarchical aspects of higher education management:

> The tensions created by the two principles are present throughout the range of institutions. While the senate or academic board may have formal power over academic matters, these are also indirectly affected by the governing body by its power to allocate between different desirable academic ends. The head of the institution may be the servant of the senate or academic board when taking the chair, but is simultaneously accountable to the governing body for running the institution.

As we shall see later in this chapter the tension between participation and accountability is a major issue in schools as well as colleges.

Democratic models in schools

The introduction of democratic approaches in schools has been slower, less complete and more piecemeal than in higher education. The tradition of all powerful heads, with authority over staff and accountability to external bodies, has stifled several attempts to develop participative modes of management in primary and secondary schools. The formal position is that heads alone are responsible for the organization and management of schools. This consideration has acted as a brake on some heads who wish to share their power and as a convenient justification for those reluctant to do so.

There are three main arguments for the participation of teaching staff in school decision-making. Firstly, there is ample evidence that teachers wish to participate more fully in the management of their schools. In part this reflects trends in the wider society towards the involvement of people in those decisions which affect their lives. Davies (1983) conducted research among fifty-one heads of departments in secondary schools which shows that they desire a higher level of involvement in decision-making. Table 4.1 gives the author's results over eight decision-making areas. Davies (1983) concludes that 'the resource management system is involving middle management to a smaller extent than they think appropriate'. This impression is confirmed by Richardson (1981) who studied the attitudes of student teachers and probationers in primary and secondary schools. He argues that 'headteachers probably underestimate the extent to which their staffs wish to participate in school decision making'.

Secondly, it can be postulated that the quality of decision-making is better where teaching staff participate in the process. Heads do not have a

Table 4.1   Head of department involvement in decisions (from Davies, 1983)

Decision-making areas	Mean score of how all the heads of dept. perceive their existing level of participation	Mean score of what all the heads of dept. think their participation should be
1. Decisions on how total resources should be allocated in the school	1.30	5.74
2. Use of school fund	1.14	5.19
3. Appointments and promotions within the department head's department	4.46	6.40
4. Use of community based funds, e.g. P.T.A. funds	1.02	4.92
5. Stock ordering and equipment	6.95	7.00
6. Curriculum design for the overall school	2.83	6.70
7. Curriculum design for their particular department	6.19	6.90
8. Allocation of staff to classes	5.96	6.82

Note: 1 = no participation; 7 = full participation

monopoly of wisdom or vision and the involvement of other staff increases the fund of experience and expertise brought to bear on problems. Participation tends to increase the job satisfaction of those involved and leads to a greater commitment to the policies of the school. Whitaker (1983, p. 54–55), a former primary head, claims that:

> there is likely to be an improvement in the quality of decisions made if all those involved in the life of the school have the opportunity to participate in solving problems relevant to them [. . .] decision-making can become a positive and dynamic force in the school.

Finally, the participation of teaching staff is important because they usually have the responsibility of implementing changes in policy. Teachers enjoy considerable discretion in their classroom activities. This is a product of their professional status with its in-built assumptions of competence to direct the learning process without close supervision. Yet heads have a responsibility to ensure curriculum coordination throughout the school. Increasingly heads have involved teachers in curriculum development if only to improve the prospects of staff implementing any policy changes. Brown (1983) argues that curriculum change in the primary school requires the active involvement of staff: 'Managing the curriculum has to stem from agreed aims and a philosophical stance that is generally accepted by the teachers'.

The recognition that greater teacher involvement may be to the benefit of schools has resulted in the emergence of a wide range of consultative and participative mechanisms. While they all represent modifications of the hierarchic approaches discussed in Chapter 3 it would be inappropriate to regard them all as democratic models. In many schools the head consults with colleagues but reserves the right to make the final decision. Whitaker (1983, p. 54–55) identifies six possible arrangements for decision-making in the primary school, ranging from autocratic to democratic:

1. The head alone controls the decision-making process by making the decisions and then announcing them to the staff who are expected to comply.
2. The head still controls the process but having made a decision attempts to give reasons for it.
3. The head undertakes the early stages of the process then recommends to staff the preferred solution. Some modification to the proposals as a result of discussion will be allowed.
4. The head invites colleagues to share in the (early) stages but then makes the final decision.

5. The head involves the staff at all stages but defines the criteria determining the choice of solution.
6. The head becomes an equal member of a corporate decision-making body.

Whitaker's classification leaves open the question of which teachers should be included in the process of consultation or participation. In certain schools there are formal arrangements for the discussion of policy issues but often membership is on an *ex officio* basis which limits the democratic aspect of the process. 'Sageton' comprehensive school provides one example of this approach.

> The heads of department together with the heads of the three schools (upper, middle and lower), the second mistress, deputy heads and headmaster of the school meet at least once a term to discuss the general running of the school and of the teaching aspects in particular. They constitute an academic board. (Evans 1983, p. 348)

While such approaches broaden the policy-making process they fall short of the requirements of a truly democratic model. Democracy implies the involvement of all teaching staff either through direct involvement in decision-making or through the opportunity to elect representatives to the policy-making body. An example of a democratic approach is provided by the management arrangements in operation at Countesthorpe college in Leicestershire. The former head of the college outlines the main features of the participative management style adopted at Countesthorpe:

> Probably most heads today would claim that their decisions are made in consultation, either with their deputies, some form of cabinet of faculty or pastoral heads, or even with their whole staff. Yet none of this consultation constitutes participatory government in the sense in which I wish to speak of it, and which has been practised at Countesthorpe since it opened in 1970. [. . .] The major policy decisions that have shaped the curriculum and discipline of the school have been made by the consensus of the staff. Increasingly, students have contributed to this consensus, and in some instances parents and governors have participated. I accepted the headship in 1972 because I found the policies and the means of determining them attractive, and was prepared to answer for them externally while being accountable internally to the college. I remain as long as those two zones of accountability are compatible.
>
> Within the college we have varied executive roles, many of them held interchangeably by staff other than myself and deputies, but without the conventional chain of authority. Our chain of authority links decision-making groups whose composition is not fixed. The body that establishes any ruling consensus is a general meeting, the Moot, which is open to all, including nonteaching staff and students. The Moot establishes its own constitution,

procedures, and chairmanship. It meets as necessary, about once in six weeks. Other decision-making groups are responsible directly or indirectly to the Moot and any individual may challenge their decisions through the Moot.

The subgroups may be standing or *ad hoc*. The principal standing committee consists of one quarter of the staff with student representation and it holds office for one quarter of the year. Thus every member of staff has a period on committee. Standing committee meets every Monday after school to receive reports and take intermediary decisions. It issues minutes the following day. Other committees include finance committee which is elected annually to make and apply the budget, and *ad hoc* appointment committees set up with each vacancy to select whoever is finally recommended to the authority for appointment to staff. All meetings are advertised and open.

Stated this way, structures appear to dominate. In operation, all depends on the attitudes of the participants, their readiness to use, and if necessary, to modify the structures in order to exercise and take responsibility for powers placed in their hands through them. [. . .] The Moot may finally decide major policy and organization, but in the preparatory ferment, the ideas may spring from any source. Working parties which eventually formulate proposals for development are open to all. Anyone may put forward a scheme. It will be tested for its desirability and practicality under the constraints of resources, staffing, space, and money. A final proposal will be the work of many hands, a modification of many ideas. Once it is ratified, though, everyone is committed to making it work, because no one has had it imposed from above without opportunity to shape it. (Watts, 1976, pp. 127, 130–131)

The Countesthorpe approach incorporates all the key elements of democratic models. The teachers' authority of expertise is acknowledged by the inclusion of all staff in the major decision-making arenas. There is an assumption that decisions can be made by consensus and that the common values of staff will avoid breakdown of the system. Above all it is a normative approach because it reflects Watts' vision that participation is the most appropriate way to determine policy.

Democratic models: goals, structure, environment and leadership

Democratic models assume that members of an organization agree on its *goals*. There is a belief that staff have a shared view of the purposes of the institution. Agreement on aims is perhaps the key element in all participative approaches to school and college management. Livingstone (1974, p. 22) outlines the functions of institutional objectives.

First of all, goals provide a general guide to activity. A member of an organisation who is aware of the organisation's goal is better able to make his activities relevant to achieving it. Secondly, goals serve as a source of legitimacy. Activities can be justified if they can be shown to further achievement of the goals. Thirdly, they are a means of measuring success. [. . .] An organisation is effective if it achieves its objectives.

The significance of agreed goals as a basis for school policies and activities is stressed by Watts (1976, pp. 133–134) in his discussion of Countesthorpe college.

[. . .] the participatory system depends upon an initial agreement of aims. That is why it is very doubtful whether an existing school could go over to a participatory approach. [. . .] Countesthorpe was made possible by the first head's clear announcement of intention which enabled him to recruit a staff who wanted to work in that way. With head and staff agreed on basics, any conflicts can be resolved by open discussion with reference to them, provided all parties learn to tolerate conflict, use it to identify issues and make compromises in order to reach consensus.

There is a clear indication here that agreement on goals, central to the ethos of democratic models, is likely to be achieved only under certain conditions. One circumstance, identified by Watts, is where staff have been chosen by the head and are likely to have similar objectives. Tipton (1973) suggests that another consideration is the background of the staff. Where this is relatively homogeneous there is a better prospect of agreement than in those institutions which exhibit substantial diversity of background. In universities and colleges the various disciplines often have rather different ideas about the central purposes of their institution. In these circumstances, as Baldridge et al. (1978, pp. 20–21) demonstrate, agreement on aims may be achieved only by obfuscation:

Most organisations know what they are doing. [. . .] By contrast, colleges and universities have vague, ambiguous goals. [. . .] As long as goals are left ambiguous and abstract, people agree; as soon as they are concretely specified and put into operation, disagreement arises.

The acknowledgement of possible conflict over the goals of educational institutions threatens to remove one of the central planks of democratic models. The belief that staff can always reach agreement over institutional purposes and policies lies at the heart of all participative approaches. Any recognition of goal conflict serves to reduce the validity of all democratic perspectives.

Democratic models share with formal approaches the view that organizational *structure* is an objective fact which has a clear meaning for all members of the institution. The major difference concerns the relationships between different elements of the structure. Formal models present structures as vertical or hierarchical with decisions being made by leaders and then passed down the structure. Subordinates are accountable to superiors for the satisfactory performance of their duties. In democratic models structures are assumed to be lateral or horizontal with participants having an equal right to determine policy and influence decisions.

In education democratic approaches are often manifested through systems of committees, which may be elaborate in the larger and more complex institutions. The decision-making process inside committees is thought to be egalitarian with influence dependent more on specific expertise than on official position. The assumption is that decisions are reached by consensus or compromise rather than acquiescence to the views of the head or principal.

There are several difficulties in assessing the nature of relationships between the organization and its *environment*. Democratic models characterize decision-making as a participative process with all members of the institution having an equal opportunity to influence policy and action. Where decisions emerge from an often complex committee system it is no easy task to establish responsibility for organizational policy. Noble and Pym (1970, pp. 435–436) point to some of the elusive qualities of decision-making by committee:

> The most striking feature of the organisation to the newcomer or outsider seeking some response from it is the *receding locus of power*. In complex organisations in the spheres of education, industry, administration or commerce, this Kafkaesque experience is very common; wherever or at whatever level one applies to the organisation, the "real" decisions always seem to be taken somewhere else.

The ambiguity of the decision-making process within democratic organizations creates a particular problem in terms of accountability to external bodies. Individuals and groups outside the institution often behave as if the head or principal has total control over the activities of other members of the organization and can be held responsible personally for its decisions. Consider this assessment of the external expectations of universities, probably the most impervious of educational institutions:

> [. . .] the central authorities themselves act on the assumption that their requests, or guidance, or prescriptions, will be followed, provided that they only address themselves to a visibly nodal point of authority in an institution. [. . .] Members of the public, too, may write to a vice-chancellor complaining of some statement made by an individual member of staff, or of the behaviour

of a group of students, as if he can unequivocally exercise managerial authority. (Becher and Kogan, 1980, p. 64)

In education, then, the head or principal is invariably held responsible for the policies of the school or college. The assumptions of formal models are in line with these expectations. Leaders are thought to determine or strongly influence decisions and are then held to be accountable to external bodies for the outcomes of policies. Democratic approaches do not fit comfortably with these formal accountability assumptions. Are heads expected to justify school policies determined within a participatory framework even where they do not enjoy their personal support? Or is the reality rather that democratic policy-making is limited in practice by the head's responsibility to external agencies? Heads must agree with, or at minimum acquiesce in, decisions made in committee if they are not to be placed in a very difficult position. The principal of Cambridgeshire College of Arts and Technology acknowledges the delicacy of such relationships:

> Roy Helmore [. . .] sees that his own credibility depends on his being able to 'carry' the academic board most of the time. If there were strong disagreements between his view and that of the academic board, he recognises that he would need to go to the governors and report in his capacity as chairman of the academic board and, differently, as principal; he recognises that this might result in a vote of no confidence by the academic board and appreciates that very few principals would be likely to survive this. (Bush and Goulding, 1984, p. 18)

Democratic theories tend to overlook the possibility of conflict between internal participative processes and external accountability. The often bland assumption that issues can be resolved by consensus leads to the comfortable conclusion that heads are always in agreement with decisions and experience no difficulty in explaining them to external bodies. In practice it may be that the head's accountability leads to a substantially modified version of democracy in most schools. There is also the risk of tension for the head who is caught between the conflicting demands of participation and accountability.

> Under present conditions ultimate responsibility for a school's performance resides with the head. However committed he may be to shared or participatory processes, he remains responsible for outcomes. Management implies responsibility, and both assume a freedom to exercise judgement and authority. If the disjunction is too great, then the possibility of ineffectiveness and stress is enhanced. (Taylor, 1983, p. 274)

In democratic models the style of *leadership* is strongly influenced by the nature of the decision-making process. Because policy is determined within a participative framework the head or principal has to adopt strategies which acknowledge that issues may emerge from different parts of the organization and are resolved in a complex interactive process. Heroic models of leadership are inappropriate when influence and power are widely distributed within the institution. Baldridge *et al.* (1978, p. 45) assess the role of the senior manager in higher education.

> The collegial leader is at most a 'first among equals' in an academic organisa- tion supposedly run by professional experts [. . .] The basic idea of the collegial leader is less to command than to listen, less to lead than to gather expert judgements, less to manage than to facilitate, less to order than to persuade and negotiate [. . .] the collegial leader is not so much a star standing alone as the developer of consensus among the professionals who must share the burden of the decision.

Democratic theorists tend to ascribe the following qualities to leaders in schools and colleges:

1. They are responsive to the needs and wishes of their professional colleagues. Heads and principals acknowledge the expertise and skill of the teachers and seek to harness these assets for the benefit of the pupils and students. Invariably they have been appointed to leadership posts after a long period as successful practitioners. Their experience makes them 'sensitive to the informal codes of professional practice which govern expectations for relations among teachers and between teachers and head' (Coulson, 1985).
2. Democratic heads seek to create formal and informal opportunities for the testing and elaboration of policy initiatives. This is done to encour- age innovation and to maximise the acceptability of school decisions. As Brown (1983, p. 224) suggests in relation to primary schools:

   > the headteacher who perceives his role as being that of a democrat [. . .] ensures that school organisation facilitates frequent staff discussion and co-ordination in order that decisions are made as a collective art.

3. Democratic models emphasize the authority of expertise rather than official authority. It follows that authority in professional organizations like schools or colleges resides as much with the staff as with the head alone. Instead of exerting authority over subordinates the leader seeks rather to influence the decisions and actions of professional colleagues. It is a more subtle and less conclusive approach than that of the formal leader.

The head or principal, then, is typified as the facilitator of an essentially participative internal process. However, as Winkley (1983) points out, 'valuing democracy does not absolve the head from the problem of initiating leadership'. Heads and principals have the major responsibility for communicating and interpreting external requirements to the internal decision-making bodies. They also bear the burden of explaining and justifying policy and action to parents, employers, education officers and other external groups and individuals. This gives them a pivotal role in the management of the institution and enables them to exercise considerable influence over its direction as long as they retain the confidence and support of their professional colleagues. For Handy (1977, p. 186) this is the essential difference between formal approaches and democratic leadership, which depends on consent.

> [. . .] the distinction between the organisation of consent and the traditional hierarchical organisation is that authority in the former is granted by those below whereas in the hierarchical state authority is conferred by those above. Your official role in the organisation of consent gives you little effective power – that is only won by the consent of those you seek to manage. Nor does this consent, once given, hold good for all time or for all circumstances. It needs constant ratification.

The limitations of democratic models

Democratic models tend to be highly normative and idealistic. Their advocates believe that participative approaches represent the most appropriate means of conducting affairs in educational institutions. Teachers exhibit that authority of expertise which justifies their involvement in the decision-making process. In addition they are able to exercise sufficient discretion in their classroom work to ensure that innovation depends on their cooperation. Democratic theorists argue that support for change is more likely to be forthcoming where teachers have been able to contribute to the process of policy formulation. However, critics of participative models point to a number of flaws which serve to limit their validity in schools and colleges. There are perhaps nine significant weaknesses of democratic perspectives.

1. Democratic models are so strongly *normative* that they tend to obscure rather than portray reality. Ideas about the most appropriate ways of managing educational institutions mingle with descriptions of behaviour. The prescriptive beliefs jostle with the analytical statements. It is not

sufficient simply to claim that participation is the dominant mode of decision-making in schools and colleges. The evidence needed to support such views tends to be sketchy and incomplete. Baldridge *et al.* (1978, p. 33) present a powerful critique of collegial models in higher education which could well be applied also to democratic approaches in schools:

> The collegial literature often confuses *descriptive* and *normative* enterprises. Are the writers saying that the university *is* a collegium or that it *ought* to be a collegium? Frequently, the discussions of collegium are more a lament for paradise lost than a description of present reality. Indeed, the collegial idea of round table decision making does not accurately reflect the actual processes in most institutions.

2. Democratic approaches to decision-making tend to be *slow and cumbersome*. When policy proposals require the approval of a series of committees the process is often tortuous and time consuming. The participative ethic requires that a decision is made by agreement where possible rather than resorting to a voting process. The attempts to achieve consensus may lead to procedural delays such as a reference back to the sponsoring committee, perhaps for further information, or consultation with other committees, individuals or external agencies. Participants may have to endure many lengthy meetings before issues are resolved. This requires patience and a considerable investment of time.

The sheer length of the democratic process may be a major factor in the relatively limited adoption of participative approaches in schools, especially those in the primary sector. Most staff are engaged in classroom activities for much or all of the day. Meetings tend to be held after school when staff are tired and ready for anything but a long-drawn-out attempt to achieve consensus on an aspect of school policy. One former primary head is unequivocal about democratic decision-making: 'Under present primary school conditions there is not enough time available to make such a system workable' (Whitaker, 1983).

3. Democratic processes can be effective only if participation is maintained at an adequate level. Just as local democracy is undermined because less than half the electorate turn out to vote so democracy in eduation is compromised if most staff choose not to participate. Given the commitment of time required of participants, levels of involvement may be inadequate to sustain democracy. Bullock (1980, p. 24) discusses reasons for nonparticipation in a working party system established at a new comprehensive school.

90% of the staff were members of Working Parties during the first academic year of their existence; but after three years only 40% of the staff were members. [. . .] A variety of reasons were given by staff for not participating in the Working Party scheme. Domestic commitments was the standard official reason given. Among the more interesting 'unofficial' reasons were that being a party member consumed so much time that lesson preparation was curtailed, especially in practical subjects. For others, opting out was a means of criticising the system, and for the more experienced staff the outcome of many hours of talk was a foregone conclusion. [. . .] It is inevitable that some staff will wish to opt out of a participatory decision making system, but a dialogue must be maintained with them to prevent isolationism and cynicism sapping staff morale and jeopardising potential innovation.

4. A further criticism of democratic perspectives is the elitist view that decisions may be made by people who *lack relevant experience or expertise*. Involvement in committees often arises through a process of election or, more simply, through individuals volunteering their services. These mechanisms do not guarantee competence relevant to the issues under discussion. A related consideration may be that inexperienced teachers find difficulties in addressing topics of school-wide concern. These factors may limit the effectiveness of participatory decision-making but the involvement of nonspecialists and less experienced staff is a necessary concomitant of democracy. Attempts to confine participation to individuals who achieve certain levels of experience or competence militate against the essence of democratic models.

5. A fundamental assumption of democratic models is that decisions are reached by consensus. It is suggested that the outcome of debate is agreement based on the shared values of participants. In practice, though, committee members have their own views and there is no guarantee of unanimity on outcomes. In addition participants often represent constituencies within the school or college. Individuals may be members of committees as representatives of the English department or the science faculty. Inevitably these sectional interests have a considerable influence on the nature of discussion in committees. Indeed the participatory framework may become the focal point of disagreement between factions. Baldridge *et al.* (1978, pp. 33–34) suggest that democratic models greatly underestimate the significance of conflict within education:

> The collegial model [. . .] fails to deal adequately with the problem of *conflict* [. . . it] neglects the prolonged battles that precede consensus and the fact that the consensus actually represents the prevalence of one group over another.

Collegial proponents are correct in declaring that simple bureaucratic rule making is not the essence of decision making, but in making this point they take the equally indefensible position that major decisions are reached primarily by consensus.

6. Democratic models have to be evaluated in relation to the special features of educational institutions. The participative aspects of decision-making exist alongside the structural and bureaucratic components of schools and colleges. Often there is tension between these rather different modes of management. Ebbutt (1976) claims in relation to further education that 'the introduction of academic boards introduces a representative element into an hierarchical structure, and [. . .] these two are incompatible'. The participative element rests on the authority of expertise possessed by professional staff but this rarely trumps the formal authority of official leaders. As Lortie (1969) suggests, 'it seems unlikely that collegial ties play a major part in reducing the potency of hierarchical authority'. The ideal of democracy may succumb to the reality of bureaucratic power.

7. Participative approaches to school and college decision-making may be difficult to sustain in view of the requirement that heads and principals remain accountable to the LEA and other external groups. Participation represents the internal dimension of democracy. Accountability may be thought of as the external aspect of democracy. Groups with a legitimate interest in school or college outcomes include parents and employers as well as local politicians and officials. These stakeholders seek explanations of policy and invariably turn to the head or principal for answers to their questions. Heads may experience considerable difficulty in defending policies which have emerged from a participative process but do not enjoy their personal support. Yet if this consideration is introduced into the internal decision-making process it serves to limit the validity of participation. The recognition of the importance of accountability leads inevitably to the conclusion that in educational institutions there cannot be more than a conditional democracy.

8. Where participation is devalued by the emphasis given to accountability and the formal authority of leaders it may lead to cynicism and apathy among staff. Teachers' reluctance to become involved in corporate decision-making is likely to be enhanced by any suspicion that the democracy is spurious. Evans's (1983, pp. 351, 353) study of 'Sageton' comprehensive school demonstrates the adverse consequences of a contradiction between democratic pretensions and bureaucratic realities.

These highly representative procedures established by the headmaster were repeatedly enshrined in a supporting rhetoric which stressed open government and easy access. [. . .] However despite the construction of these elaborate mechanisms for participation and representation there persisted much evidence to suggest a widespread disaffection and disenchantment with the opportunities presented for involvement in policy formation and decision making. [. . .] A feeling was being expressed that such occasions had a great deal more to do with the dissemination of policies predetermined by the head [. . .] than providing genuine opportunity for all staff to influence [their] formation.

9. Democratic processes in schools depend crucially on the attitudes of heads. In colleges the academic board provides a legitimate forum for the involvement of staff in decision-making and principals have to recognize and work with this alternative power source. In schools participative machinery can be established only with the support of the head, who can also strongly influence the topics to be discussed and exercise a veto on unpalatable decisions. While wise heads take account of the views of their staff, a process which relies on the voluntary agreement of the leader falls short of a true democracy. This is a key test of the significance of democratic models in schools, as Harling (1980) makes clear: 'Can participation really be valid if its existence depends on the beneficence of the head, as indeed it must given the present structure of primary education?'

Democratic models introduce some key considerations into the discussion of educational management. Their advocates are right to point to the significance of the authority of expertise possessed by professional staff. In addition teachers have sufficient discretion in their classroom work to ensure that many policy changes cannot succeed without their consent. Participative approaches are a necessary antidote to the rigid hierarchical assumptions of the formal models. However, democratic perspectives provide an incomplete picture of management in education. In schools in particular these theories underestimate the official authority of the head and present bland assumptions of consensus which often cannot be substantiated. Collegial models originated in higher education and remain important normative statements of management in universities, polytechnics and colleges. Their validity is challenged, however, by those who prefer to emphasize conflict rather than consensus. Baldridge *et al.* (1978, p. 17) were among the first writers to focus on sectionalism and power rather than professional authority and they conclude that even in higher education democratic models are now of limited relevance.

Collegial management is probably dying – if it ever existed at all. [. . .]

Collegiality, the ideal of so many, was probably never dominant in modern higher education outside of a few departmental activities. But social trends will probably undermine even the limited collegial influence that once existed.

References

Baldridge, J.V., Curtis, D.V., Ecker, G. and Riley, G.L. (1978) *Policy Making and Effective Leadership*, Jossey Bass, San Francisco

Becher, T. and Kogan, M. (1980) *Process and Structure in Higher Education*, Gower, Aldershot

Brown, C.M. (1983) Curriculum management in the junior school, *School Organisation*, Vol. 3, No. 3, pp. 221–228

Bullock, A.W. (1980) Teacher participation in school decision making, *Cambridge Journal of Education*, Vol. 10, No. 1, pp 21–28

Bush, T. and Goulding, S. (1984) *Cambridgeshire College of Arts and Technology: facing the cuts*, E324 Management in Post Compulsory Education, Block 3, Part 4, Open University Press, Milton Keynes

Coulson, A. (1985) *The Managerial Behaviour of Primary School Heads*, Collected Original Resources in Education, Carfax Publishing Company, Abingdon

Davies, B. (1983) Head of department involvement in decisions, *Educational Management and Administration*, Vol. 11, No. 3, pp. 173–176

Department of Education and Science (1966) *Report of the Study Group on the Government of Colleges of Education* (The Weaver Report), HMSO, London

Ebbutt, K. (1976) A study of academic boards in institutions of further education in the light of Rex's conflict theory, M.Phil. Thesis, University of London

Evans, J. (1983) Decision-making, conflict and control in comprehensive schooling: the management or harassment of curriculum reform, *School Organisation*, Vol. 3, No. 4, pp 345–360

Glatter, R. (1984) *Managing for Change*, E324 Management in Post Compulsory Education, Block 6, Open University Press, Milton Keynes

Handy, C.B. (1983) The organisations of consent. In D.W. Piper and R. Glatter (Eds.) *The Changing University*, NFER-Nelson, Windsor

Harling, P. (1980) School decision-making and the primary headteacher, *Education 3–13*, Vol. 8, No. 2, pp 44–48

Kogan, M. (1984) *Models and Structures*, E324 Management in Post Compulsory Education, Block 3, Part 1, Open University Press, Milton Keynes

Livingstone, H. (1974) *The University: An Organisational Analysis*, Blackie, Glasgow

Lortie, D.C. (1969) The balance of control and autonomy in elementary school teaching. In A. Etzioni (Ed.) *The Semi-Professions and Their Organisation*, Free Press, a division of Macmillan Inc., New York

Moodie, G.C. and Eustace, R. (1974) *Power and Authority in British Universities*, George Allen and Unwin, London

Noble, T. and Pym, B. (1970) Collegial authority and the receding locus of power, *British Journal of Sociology*, Vol. 21, pp 431–445

Richardson, G.A. (1981) Student–teacher attitudes towards decision-making in schools before and after taking up their first appointments, *Educational Studies*, Vol. 7, No. 1, pp 7–15

Richman, B.M. and Farmer, R.N. (1974) *Leadership, Goals and Power in Higher Education*, Jossey Bass, San Francisco

Taylor, K. (1983) Heads and the freedom to manage, *School Organisation*, Vol. 3, No. 3, pp 273–286

Tipton, B.F.A. (1973) *Conflict and Change in a Technical College*, Hutchinson, London

Watts, J. (1976) Sharing it out: the role of the head in participatory government. In R.S. Peters (Ed.) *The Role of the Head*, Routledge and Kegan Paul, London, pp 127–136

Whitaker, P. (1983) *The Primary Head*, Heinemann, London © Patrick Whitaker 1983. Reprinted by permission of Heinemann Educational Books Ltd., London

Williams, G. and Blackstone, T. (1983) *Response to Adversity*, Society for Research into Higher Education, Guildford

Winkley, D. (1983) An analytical view of primary school leadership, *School Organisation*, Vol. 3, No. 1, pp 15–26

CHAPTER 5

POLITICAL MODELS

Central features of political models

Political models embrace those theories which characterize decision-making as a bargaining process. They assume that organizations are political arenas whose members engage in political activity in pursuit of their interests. Analysis focuses on the distribution of power and influence in organizations and on the bargaining and negotiation between interest groups. Conflict is regarded as endemic within organizations and management is directed towards the regulation of political behaviour. The definition suggested below incorporates the main elements of these approaches:

> Political models assume that in organizations policy and decisions emerge through a process of negotiation and bargaining. Interest groups develop and form alliances in pursuit of particular policy objectives. Conflict is viewed as a natural phenomenon and power accrues to dominant coalitions rather than being the preserve of formal leaders.

Politics tend to be regarded as the concern of central and local government and to be associated strongly with the political parties who compete for our votes at general and local elections. It is useful to loosen this close identity between government and politics before seeking to apply political metaphors to educational institutions. It is the essence of these perspectives that political behaviour occurs naturally in all organizations, both formal and informal. Mackenzie (1967, p. 156) explains why politics merit wider consideration:

> [. . .] both political scientists and plain men feel that what they meet in the politics of the state turns up again in the politics of the club, the office, the

army unit and even the family. What generates political interest in all this range of institutions is that we think we can feel politics in them, and that we cannot describe them adequately without using political concepts.

The relevance of political models to educational institutions is given increasing recognition by both academics and practitioners. Within education these perspectives are often referred to as 'micropolitics'. Glatter (1982, p. 161) claims that micropolitics is 'an essential perspective':

> The language of power, coalitions, arenas, contests, bargaining, negotiations, interests, ambiguity and so on seems very helpful in distinguishing rhetoric from reality [. . .] in drawing attention to the different purposes which different individuals, groups and institutions have and the various ways they set about attaining them. [. . .] the approaches which may be broadly termed the micropolitical perspective are essential to an understanding of educational administration and management.

Political models have the following major features:

1. They tend to focus on *group activity* rather than the institution as an entity. The emphasis is on the basic unit (Becher and Kogan, 1980) not the school or college level. Interaction between groups is at the heart of political approaches whereas formal and democratic models stress the institutional level. 'The basic unit of traditional political analysis is the sub group [. . .] the basic unit of an apolitical perspective is the total system' (Bacharach and Lawler, 1980).

In education much of the political analysis centres on the influence of academic departments. Marland (1982, pp. 122–123) refers to 'the traditional political power of heads of departments' and deprecates their sectional approach to school policy-making:

> The status and self esteem of heads of departments seems to be increased the narrower the view and decreased if they develop a broader vision. For instance members of a subject department will sharply criticise their head of department if she or he does not push unremittingly for the self interest of the department. Thus, the good team leader is felt by the team as one who demands adamantly, ostentatiously, and consistently for more teachers, more space, more money, more equipment, more rooms, more pupils, smaller groups, and, above all, more of the pupils' time.

The department is also a powerful influence on the management of universities and colleges, as Clark (1983) makes clear: 'Basic to the action patterns of higher education systems is their organisation around disciplines.'

2. Political models are concerned with *interests* and *interest groups*.

Individuals are thought to have a variety of interests which they pursue within the organization. Hoyle (1982, p. 89) distinguishes between personal, professional and political interests and points to the development of interest groups in education:

> Interests are pursued by individuals but frequently they are most effectively pursued in collaboration with others who share a common concern. Some of these may have the qualities of a group in that they are relatively enduring and have a degree of cohesion, but others [. . .] will be looser associations of individuals who collaborate only infrequently when a common interest comes to the fore.

The more permanent interest groups, such as departments, are cohesive because of shared values and beliefs. The individuals within such groups have common attitudes towards many of the central issues in schools and colleges. Because these interest groups have different goals and values, institutions tend to be fragmented rather than the united organizations portrayed in formal and democratic models. On particular issues groups may form alliances to press for policies which relate to their joint interests. These coalitions may well be temporary, disbanding when certain objectives have been achieved, while the interest groups often have long-term significance.

3. Political models stress the prevalence of *conflict* in organizations. Interest groups pursue their independent objectives which may be in contrast to the aims of other elements within the institution and lead to conflict between them. A key aspect of political perspectives is the view that conflict is a normal feature of organizations. Formal and democratic models have a strong harmony bias where the possibility of disagreement is ignored or assumed away. In contrast, Baldridge *et al.* (1978, p. 35) regard conflict in educational institutions as both inevitable and welcome:

> In a fragmented, dynamic social system, conflict is natural and not necessarily a symptom of breakdown in the academic community. In fact, conflict is a significant factor in promoting healthy organisational change.

4. Political perspectives assume that the *goals* of organizations are unstable, ambiguous and contested. Individuals, interest groups and coalitions have their own purposes and act towards the achievement of these objectives. Goals may be disputed and then become a significant element in the conflict between groups. Certain groups succeed in establishing their goals as the objectives of the institution while other interests seek to supplant the official purposes with their own objectives. Cyert (1975, p. 28)

discusses the nature of disagreement between interest groups and the institution:

> Within any organisation conflicts tend to arise between the goals of subunits and the overall goals of the total organisation. These conflicts frequently are based on a professional goal that the subunit desires to achieve and the resources that the organisational management is prepared to allocate toward the achievement of that goal.

Interest groups are likely to promote their objectives in a variety of ways until they receive the support of the policy-makers. This does not end the conflict because the endorsement of one set of purposes tends to be at the expense of other goals, whose proponents continue to lobby for their own ideas. Disagreement over goals is then a continuing feature of the policy process in organizations.

5. In political arenas decisions emerge after a complex process of *bargaining and negotiation*. Formal approaches assume that decisions follow a rational process. Options are evaluated in terms of the objectives of the organization and the most appropriate alternative is selected. Policy-making in political settings is a more uncertain business. Interests are promoted in committees and at numerous unofficial encounters between participants. Policies cannot be judged primarily in terms of the goals of the institution because these are subject to the same process of internal debate and subsequent change. The objectives are a moving target, as Bolman and Deal (1984, pp. 109–110) suggest:

> Organisational goals and decisions emerge from ongoing processes of bargaining, negotiation, and jockeying for position among individuals and groups [. . . Each group] wants to have an impact on organisational decisions and attempts to do so by participating in a multistage process that includes articulation of interests, efforts to get those interests translated into institutional policy, resolution of conflicting forces into an accepted policy, and implementation of decisions that have been attained.

The emphasis on the several stages of decision-making is significant because it multiplies the opportunities available to interest groups to exert influence on the policy process. Decisions on a subject at one forum do not necessarily resolve the issue because the unsuccessful groups are likely to pursue the matter whenever opportunities arise or can be engineered.

6. The concept of *power* is central to all political theories of organizations. The complex decision-making process is likely to be determined ultimately according to the relative power of the participating individuals and groups. These participants mobilize resources of power which are deployed in

support of their interests and have a significant impact on policy outcomes, as Mangham (1979, p. 17) demonstrates:

> [. . .] what underpins the decision and produces the action [. . .] is the direct result of the power and the skill of the proponents and opponents of all the action in question. Decisions and actions within organisations may be seen as the consequence of the pulling and hauling that is politics.

There are many sources of power but in broad terms a distinction can be made between authority and influence. Authority is legitimate power which is vested in leaders within formal organizations. Authority involves a legal right to make decisions which may be supported by sanctions. Influence represents an ability to affect outcomes and depends on personal character-istics and expertise. Hoyle (1982, p. 90) points to the ways in which these two aspects of power operate within educational institutions:

> Influence differs from authority in having a number of sources in the organization, in being embedded in the actual relationships between groups rather than located in an abstract legal source, and is not fixed but is variable and operates through bargaining, manipulation, exchange and so forth.
>   The head teacher in Britain has a high degree of authority; but his exercise of this authority is increasingly modified as teachers' sources of influence [. . .] increase and thus involves the head in a greater degree of exchange and bargaining behaviour.

The nature and sources of power in education are examined in more detail on page 76–78.

7. Several political theorists emphasize the significance of *external influ-ences* on internal decision-making. The political process includes inputs from outside bodies and individuals which are often mediated by the internal participants. Sergiovanni (1984, p. 6) explains the nature of the interaction between educational institutions and external groups:

> The political perspective is concerned with the dynamic interplay of the organisation with forces in its external environment. Schools and universities, for example, are viewed as open rather than closed systems, as integral parts of a larger environment not as bounded entities isolated from their environment. They receive inputs, process them, and return outputs to the environment. Inputs are presumed to be diverse and output demands often conflicting. As a result there is constant interplay between school and environment.

In this respect political approaches are similar to the open systems theories considered in Chapter 3. The major difference concerns the ways in which external pressures are imported into school or college decision-making. In formal models it is assumed that outside influences are transmitted through heads or principals whose knowledge of the external environ-ment reinforces their official authority. The leaders' interpretation of these pressures may then be a significant contribution to the decision-making process. In political models it is thought that external factors are introduced by interest groups in support of their policy objectives. In further educa-tion, for example, staff whose courses are threatened by low enrolments may cite evidence from employers who value the threatened courses. These environmental considerations mingle with the internal pressures and add to the complexity and ambiguity of decision-making.

8. Political models are particularly appropriate as ways of understanding the *distribution of resources* in educational institutions. Decisions about the allocation of resources are likely to be among the most significant aspects of the policy process in schools and colleges. Resources include not only financial assets such as capitation or equipment but also teachers and other staff. Even in periods of expansion there is competition between interest groups for additional resources. Departments want more staff, more books, more teaching time and more equipment. At times of scarce resources these demands cannot be met and there is conflict between groups which is resolved by an essentially political process. Davies and Morgan (1983, p. 168) point to the intensification of political decision-making during periods of retrenchment:

> In the formulation of policy to cope with contraction, the political 'crunch' issue is how to decide which departments grow, which remain in steady state, which contract, and which are to be immediately cut, or progressively phased out. The balance between political and rational [. . .] decision criteria shifts towards the political when resources are scarce [. . .] the relative political power of organisational subunits is more significant at a time of resource scarcity.

Several of the ideas discussed in this section are brought together in the political model outlined by Baldridge (1971). The author considers the formation of interest groups and discusses the ways in which policies emerge from the kaleidoscope of conflicting pressures (see Figure 5.1). Baldridge postulates five stages in the policy process, with particular reference to universities:

> First is a *social structure*, that is, a configuration of social groups with basically different life-styles and political interests. The crucial point is that the differences often lead to conflict, for what is in the interest of one group may damage another. It is important, then, to examine the social setting with its fragmented groups, divergent goal aspiration, and conflicting claims on

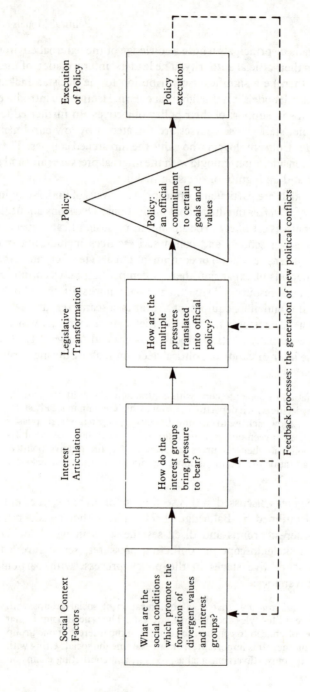

Figure 5.1 A political model (from Baldridge, 1971)

the decision makers. The university has a particularly complex pluralistic social system because many groups inside and outside the organization are pushing in various directions, according to their own special interests. One need only glance at the various outside 'publics' of a university to see its external social context, and the same glance turned inward would immediately reveal the internal social structure with its fragmented interest groups. Many of the current conflicts on the campus have their roots in the complexity of the academic social structure and in the complex goals and values held by these divergent groups.

Second is the process of *interest articulation*. Groups with conflicting values and goals must somehow translate them into effective influence if they are to obtain favorable action by legislative bodies. How does a powerful group exert its pressure, what threats or promises can it make, and how does it translate its desires into political capital? There are many forms of interest articulation at work among the policy makers from every quarter and it assumes a multitude of shapes. Political intervention comes from external groups, from faculty groups demanding authority, from rioting student groups, and from officials who apply their formal authority. In this political tangle the articulation of interests is a fundamental process.

Third is the dynamics by which articulated interests are translated into policies – the *legislative stage*. Legislative bodies respond to pressures, transforming the conflict into politically feasible policy. In the process many claims are played off against one another, negotiations are undertaken, compromises are forged, and rewards are divided. Committees meet, commissions report, negotiators bargain, and powerful people 'higgle and haggle' about the eventual policy. Not only must we identify the types of interest groups and the methods they use to bring pressure but we must also clarify the translation process by which all these pressures are negotiated into a formal policy.

Fourth, the *formulation of policy* is the end result. The articulated interests have gone through conflict and compromise stages and the final legislative action is taken. The policy is the official climax to the conflict and represents an authoritative, binding decision to commit the organization to one set of possible alternative actions, to one set of goals and values.

Finally the *execution of policy* occurs. The conflict comes to a climax, the battle is at least officially over, and the resulting policy is turned over to the bureaucrats for routine execution. Of course, this is oversimplified, but it is remarkable that yesterday's vicious battle may indeed become today's boring bureaucratic chore. This may not be the end of the matter, however, for two things are likely to happen. First, the major losers in the conflict may take up their arms again for a new round of interest articulation. Second, the execution of policy inevitably causes *a feedback cycle*, in which the policy generates new tensions, new vested interests, and a new cycle of political conflict.

In summary, the broad outlines of the political system look like this: a complex social structure generates multiple pressures, many forms of power and pressure impinge on the decision makers, a legislative stage translates these pressures into policy, and a policy execution phase finally generates feedback in the form of new conflicts. (Baldridge, 1971, pp. 23–24)

Perhaps the most significant aspect of the Baldridge model is that it is essentially iterative. The policy-making process is rarely a straightforward matter. Rather it is capable of breakdown at any stage as opposing interests coalesce to defeat proposals and substitute their own plans. This leads to the feedback processes which inevitably follow the breakdown of particular proposals. Ultimately the success or failure of interest groups in promoting their objectives depends on the resources of power which they are able to mobilize in support of their plans.

Sources of power in education

Power may be regarded as the ability to determine the behaviour of others or to decide the outcome of conflict. Where there is disagreement it is likely to be resolved according to the relative resources of power available to the participants. We noted earlier that power may arise from either authority or influence and Bacharach and Lawler (1980) identify seven distinctions between these two aspects of power.

1. Authority is the static, structural aspect of power in organizations; influence is the dynamic, tactical element.
2. Authority is the formal aspect of power; influence is the informal aspect.
3. Authority refers to the formally sanctioned right to make final decisions; influence is not sanctioned by the organization and is, therefore, not a matter of organizational rights.
4. Authority implies involuntary submission by subordinates; influence implies voluntary submission and does not necessarily entail a superior–subordinate relationship.
5. Authority flows downward, and it is unidirectional; influence is multi-directional and can flow upward, downward, or horizontally.
6. The source of authority is solely structural; the source of influence may be personal characteristics, expertise, or opportunity.
7. Authority is circumscribed, that is, the domain, scope, and legitimacy of the power are specifically and clearly delimited; influence is uncircumscribed, that is, its domain, scope, and legitimacy are typically ambiguous. (Bacharach and Lawler, 1980, p. 44)

These distinctions are valuable in considering the sources of power in educational institutions. There are five significant forms of power of particular relevance to schools and colleges:

1. A major source of power in any organization is that accruing to indi-

viduals who hold an *official position* in the institution. Formal positions confer authority on their holders, who have a recognized right to make decisions or to play a key role in the policy-making process. In schools the head is regarded as the legitimate leader and possesses legal authority which is inevitably a key determinant of school policy. Other staff who hold senior posts may also exercise positional power. These may include deputy heads, heads of department and pastoral leaders. In a hierarchy the more highly placed individuals exert the greater authority but in certain circumstances this may be countered by other forms of power.

2. In a professional organization such as a school or college there is a significant reservoir of power available to those who possess appropriate *expertise*. Educational institutions employ many staff who have specialist knowledge of particular parts of the curriculum. The music specialist, for example, is regarded as the expert and official leaders are invariably cautious in substituting their own judgements for those of their heads of department in curricular matters. In certain circumstances there may be conflict between formal leaders and experts but the outcome is by no means certain and, if the disagreement is prolonged, it may damage the coherence of the organization. Expert power should be regarded as influence rather than authority.

3. Individuals who are charismatic or possess verbal skills or certain other characteristics may be able to exercise *personal* power. Staff who are able to influence behaviour or decisions by virtue of personal abilities or qualities are often thought to possess the attributes of leadership. These personal skills are independent of the power accruing to individuals by virtue of their position in the organization. In school staff rooms, for example, there are often a few individuals who command the respect of colleagues because of their perceived wisdom or insight. These teachers may become alternative leaders whose views are sought on the key issues. According to Bacharach and Lawler (1980) leadership is primarily a product of personal qualities rather than official position: 'Leadership encompasses the personal abilities and characteristics that key individuals have apart from their offices or other sources of power.' Personal power clearly depends on influence rather than authority.

4. Power is likely to be possessed to a significant degree by individuals who have *control of rewards*. People who are able to determine the distribution of rewards are inevitably perceived as powerful by those who value such returns. In education rewards may include promotion, good references and allocation to favoured classes or groups. Individuals who control or

influence these benefits may be able to determine the behaviour of teachers who seek one or more of the rewards. Typically the head or principal is the major arbiter of promotion and references although advice may be sought from heads of department or others who possess relevant knowledge or information. Classes may be allocated by heads of department. These leaders are powerful in relation to aspiring teachers but may have little influence on those staff who choose to spurn these rewards. Control of rewards may be regarded as authority rather than influence where they emanate from the leader acting in an official capacity.

5. The mirror image of the control of rewards may be *coercive* power. This implies the ability to enforce compliance with a particular requirement. Coercion is backed by the threat of sanctions. Heads may exercise coercive power by threatening not to supply a good reference for external applications or warning about the prospects for internal promotion. In certain circumstances coercion may be used in conjunction with the control of rewards to manipulate the behaviour of others. This 'carrot and whip' combination may have a powerful double effect on staff and it is present as at least a latent consideration in all schools and colleges. In a hierarchy it is assumed that leaders have a right to seek the compliance of staff with legitimate instructions issued by superordinates. In this sense coercive power may be regarded as authority rather than influence.

Consideration of these five sources leads to the conclusion that heads and principals possess substantial resources of power. They have the capacity to determine to a considerable extent the behaviour of their colleagues. However, they do not have absolute power. There are alternative sources of influence which rest on charisma and expertise and these may counterbalance the head's formal authority.

Compliance and exchange

The power held by official leaders is reinforced each time that participants comply with their requests or instructions. Where staff decline to comply with these requirements the power of leaders is compromised and ultimately their position may be threatened. It should not be assumed that acceptance of authority or influence is automatic. Rather the recipient of the leader's imperatives may choose to accept or reject suggestions to behave in a particular way. Homans (1974, p. 2) considers the nature of the relationship between leaders and subordinates:

> [. . .] some persons give orders or their equivalent and some others obey or disobey them. The chains of command or other sorts of influence that connect members of the units together are often long and complicated, but at every link in the chain there is a person faced with the question whether he will give an order and another faced with the question whether he will obey it.

A decision to accept the order given by another person may be regarded as a submission to the power of that leader. The concept of compliance thus represents an alternative mode for analyzing power relationships in organizations. The essential difference is that the approach is centred on the recipient of instructions rather than the person who issues the orders. Etzioni (1961, pp. 21–22) defines compliance and explains its relationship to the concept of power.

> *Compliance* refers both to a relation in which an actor behaves in accordance with a directive supported by another actor's power, and to the orientation of the subordinated actor to the power applied.
> By *supported* we mean that those who have power manipulate means which they command in such a manner that certain other actors find following the directive rewarding, while not following it incurs deprivations. In this sense, compliance relations are asymmetric (or vertical). But it is not assumed that the subordinates have no power, only that they have less [. . .]
> The *orientation of the subordinated actor* can be characterised as positive (commitment) or negative (alienation). It is determined in part by the degree to which the power applied is considered legitimate by the subordinated actor, and in part by its congruence with the line of action he would desire. [. . .] In sum there are two parties to a compliance relationship: an actor who exercises power, and an actor, subject to this power, who responds to this subjection with either more or less alienation or more or less commitment.

Etzioni thus presents power and compliance as the obverse and reverse of the same coin but emphasizes that subordinates do possess power, albeit to a lesser extent than leaders. Where two parties in an organization both hold power the relationship may become more equal than is suggested by a power-compliance model. This may be especially true of professional organizations such as schools and colleges. Lortie (1969, p. 34) argues that:

> the teacher's relationship to administrative superiors can move away from subordination towards exchange. A relationship of exchange implies that the teacher can assert as well as respond to claims.

Exchange theory represents another way of approaching relationships in organizations but it is closely linked to the concept of power, as Bacharach and Lawler (1980, p. 19) suggest:

[. . .] power is a central aspect of an exchange approach to social relationships, and dependence or interdependence constitutes the point of
departure for analysing power. [. . .] Dependence is what makes exchange an
integral part of any social relationship. Without dependence, there is no
reason for an exchange, because parties can operate and obtain outcomes in
total isolation.

Exchange theory is identified with the work of Blau (1964) and Homans
(1958 and 1974). Blau defines social exchange as the 'voluntary actions of
individuals that are motivated by the returns they are expected to bring and
typically do in fact bring from others'. Homans (1958, p. 606) spells out the
nature of an exchange relationship:

Social behaviour is an exchange of goods, material goods but also non-
material ones, such as the symbols of approval or prestige. Persons that give
much to others try to get much from them, and persons that get much from
others are under pressure to give much to them. This process of influence
tends to work out at equilibrium to a balance in the exchanges.

The concept of exchange is a profitable way of examining relationships in
education. Heads and principals possess authority arising from their positions as the formal leaders of their institutions. They also hold power in the
form of key rewards such as promotion and references. However, the head
requires the cooperation of staff to secure the effective management of the
school. An exchange may secure benefit for both parties to the arrangement. Hoyle (1981) outlines the goods or rewards available to heads and
teachers engaging in a process of exchange.

The head has the following categories of 'goods' available for exchange:
- *Material resources*: The head has a high degree of control over such resources as
  books and equipment which he can distribute differentially as part of the
  exchange process. It is perhaps significant that headteachers tend not to
  democratize decisions over such allocations.
- *Promotion*: The British headteacher has a greater direct control over promotion
  than his equivalent elsewhere. His freedom to distribute scale-posts within his
  school is a powerful resource which may not be brought out openly in a
  bargaining situation but is no less potent for remaining implicit. The head has
  also a crucial role in the promotion of members of his staff to higher statuses in
  other schools since his reference will be a key factor.
- *Esteem*: The head is in a position to increase, or otherwise, the teacher's
  self-esteem and esteem in the eyes of colleagues through favourable remarks
  made privately or publicly.
- *Autonomy*: The head is in a position to determine the degree of autonomy
  enjoyed by the teacher by refraining from monitoring his teaching and other
  activities.

– *Lax application of rules*: This resource is somewhat related to autonomy. A head is in a position to insist on rules being kept to the letter, but as an implicit bargaining ploy he may be willing 'to turn a blind eye' when they are infringed. He can apply the rules differentially insisting on their observation in the case of teachers he has little regard for, but failing to do so in the case of teachers for whom he has a high regard or whose support he is seeking.

There is an imbalance between the bargaining resources of the head and of the teacher. The latter has fewer 'goods' to trade and those that he has tend to be symbolic rather than material. Nevertheless, these are important to the head and some examples are:

– *Esteem*: The private or public expression of regard for the head as a person and as a professional.
– *Support*: The acceptance of the head's aims for the school.
– *Opinion leadership*: This is related to support and involves the use of personal influence in the staff group to gain acceptance for the head's goals or authority.
– *Conformity*: The acceptance of the rules and procedures laid down by the head to the extent that he wishes them to be strictly observed. There may be a paradox here whereby the head is lax in the application of rules in those cases where the teachers are most willing to follow them.
– *Reputation*: The enhancement of the prestige of the school (and hence of the head) through examination success, sporting success, involvement in community activities, etc. (Hoyle, 1981, p. 17)

Exchanges may also occur between teachers in schools and colleges. For example one teacher may agree to support another's claim to additional resources on the understanding that the gesture is reciprocated, perhaps on a different occasion. This links back to the idea of alliances and coalitions discussed earlier in this chapter. Exchange theory is likely to be useful in understanding behaviour in many different situations in educational institutions.

Political models: goals, structure, environment and leadership

Political models differ from both the formal and democratic approaches in that they focus primarily on the *goals* of subunits rather than the objectives of the institution itself. They assume that interest groups have purposes to support and advance their interests and that they are pursued vigorously within the institution. Mangham (1979, p. 16) claims that:

[. . .] organisations may be said to consist of many groups and individuals, multiple coalitions and alliances and each acting so as to achieve its own set of goals and objectives.

Democratic approaches assume that there is agreement over the goals of the organization while political models emphasize that there is no such consensus. Schools and colleges have multiple goals reflecting the various interest groups. These groups endeavour to promote their own objectives as the official purposes of the institution. As a result goals are ambiguous, unstable and contested. Bolman and Deal (1984, p. 111) stress that organizational goals emerge from a process of bargaining and negotiation.

> Different individuals and groups have different objectives and resources, and each attempts to bargain with other members or coalitions in order to influence the goals and decision making of the system.

The capacity to secure institutional backing for group objectives depends crucially on the power of the interest group and the ability of its members to mobilize support from other subunits within the organization. There is a continuing process of negotiation and alliance building to muster sufficient support for the group's policy objectives. Goals are unstable because alliances break down and new factors are introduced into the bargaining process. The extant objectives may be usurped by purposes advanced by new coalitions of interests.

Political models assume that organizational *structure* emerges from the process of bargaining and negotiation and may be subject to change as the interest groups jockey for position. Formal and democratic approaches present structure as a stable aspect of the organization while political theories regard it as one of the uncertain and conflictual elements of the institution. The structure is developed not so much for organizational effectiveness, as formal theorists suggest, but rather to determine which interests are to be served by the organization. A management team drawn primarily from heads of department, for example, may be seen as a device to reinforce their baronial power. Bolman and Deal (1984, p. 141) argue that structure is simply one element in the constant pattern of negotiation among the subunits: 'So the groups agree on ways of dividing up power and resources, and those divisions are reflected in the design of the organisation.'

The different parts of the structure, once established, are portrayed as potential battlegrounds where the interest groups engage in combat to secure the supremacy of their policy objectives. The various committees and more informal groups are settings for the continuing conflict between participants, as the research conducted by Ebbutt and Brown (1978, p. 8) confirms:

Each of the staff interviewed at colleges A, B and C was asked whether in his opinion the academic board was an independent body making decisions in a coherent way with a mind of its own and on its own initiative, or whether it was more a forum in which competing interests within the college sought to get their own way through bargaining and adjustment. The answers given tended towards the latter view, which was also the author's impression from the documents recording the consultative process.

In political models relationships between organizations and their *environments* are typified as unstable and ambiguous in a similar way to that postulated for internal decision-making. External forces are portrayed as interest groups which contribute to the complex pattern of negotiation and bargaining thought to characterize policy formation in schools and colleges. Baldridge *et al.* (1978, p. 36) stress the significance of outside interests:

> External interest groups exert a great deal of influence over the policy making process. And external pressures and formal control by outside agencies [. . .] are powerful shapers of internal governance processes.

The various groups which have an interest in educational institutions tend to have rather different motivations for their involvement and to employ different methods of applying pressure to schools and colleges. Official bodies are concerned about the institution's educational standards and exert their authority through the head or principal. Unofficial groups usually have more sectional interests to pursue. Employers may want the school to instil particular skills while parents understandably focus on the progress of their own children. These pressures may be transmitted through the teachers most involved with their interests rather than via the leader. Political theories emphasize the importance of these informal processes, as Baldridge *et al.* (1978, p. 21) suggest:

> Society feeds clients with specific needs into the institution and the institution acts upon them and then returns them to the larger society. This is an extremely important fact, for the clients demand and often obtain a significant amount of influence over the decision making processes of the institution. Even powerless clients such as small school children usually have protectors such as parents who demand a voice in the operation of the organisation.

There are two central facets of *leadership* within political arenas. In the first place the head or principal is a key participant in the process of bargaining and negotiation. Leaders have their own values, interests and policy objectives which they seek to advance at appropriate opportunities in committees and informal settings. Heads have substantial reserves of power which they deploy in support of their personal and institutional goals. In particular they have the major responsibility for communicating and interpreting the views of many of the external groups. Leaders also have a significant influence on the nature of the internal decision-making process and may exercise a controlling effect on the proceedings of committees. At one college examined by Ebbutt and Brown (1978), 'there was general agreement that the principal manipulated the agenda items, and even the minutes to some extent, to suit himself'.

Secondly, heads have a responsibility to sustain the viability of the institution and to promote the conditions within which policies can be tested and, ultimately, receive the endorsement of the various interest groups. To achieve acceptable courses of action leaders become mediators who attempt to build coalitions in support of policies. There is a recurring pattern of discussion with representatives of power blocks to secure a measure of agreement. This may involve concessions and compromises so that the more powerful groups achieve benefits in exchange for their support:

> Management can then be seen as a process of engaging in or regulating conflict, bargaining, power and exchange. Political models therefore emphasize the scope for managerial discretion in determining objectives. A prerequisite for effectiveness is that the purposes of powerful individuals or groups within the organisation are satisfactorily met. (Cuthbert, 1984, p. 53)

The limitations of political models

Political models are primarily descriptive and analytical approaches which give valuable insights into the operation of educational institutions. The focus on interests and the conflict between groups offer a persuasive interpretation of the decision-making process in schools and colleges. For many teachers the emphasis on power as the major determinant of policy outcomes is convincing and fits their day-to-day experience better than any other model. Bolman and Deal (1984, p. 144) argue that for many people political models capture several of the essential features of institutions.

> For them, the political frame presents the only realistic portrayal of organisations [. . .] The political frame says that power and politics are central to organisations and cannot be swept under the rug. The perspective represents an important antidote to the antiseptic rationality sometimes present in structural analysis.

Although political approaches are recognized as plausible and valuable ways of understanding organizations they have several limitations when applied to schools and colleges. The four major criticisms are probably the following:

1. Political models are immersed so strongly in the language of power, conflict and manipulation that they neglect other standard aspects of organizations. There is little attempt to discuss the various processes of management or any real acknowledgement that most organizations operate for much of the time according to routine bureaucratic procedures. The focus is heavily on policy formulation while the implementation of policy receives little attention. Political perspectives probably understate the significance of organizational structure as a constraint on the nature of political activity. The outcomes of bargaining and negotiation are endorsed, or may falter, within the formal authority structure of the school or college. Baldridge is widely recognized as the leading writer on the application of political models to education but he acknowledges that modifications are required to accommodate certain aspects of the more formal approaches:

> [. . .] our original political model probably underestimated the impact of routine bureaucratic processes. Many decisions are made not in the heat of political controversy but because standard operating procedures dominate in most organizations. [. . .] the model downplayed long-term patterns of decision processes and neglected the way institutional structure shaped and channelled political efforts. (Baldridge *et al.*, 1978, pp. 42–43)

2. Political models stress the influence of interest groups on decision-making and give little attention to the institutional level. The assumption is that organizations are fragmented into groups which pursue their own independent goals. These subunits compete to establish the supremacy of their policy objectives and to secure their endorsement within the institution. This aspect of political models may be inappropriate for most primary schools which do not have a departmental structure or other apparatus which could be a focal point for political activity. Smaller schools may have only a few class teachers and a head, who may also be a class teacher. The institutional level may be the centre of attention for staff in these schools, invalidating the emphasis given to interest group fragmentation in political models.

3. In political models there is too much emphasis on conflict and a neglect of the possibility of professional collaboration leading to agreed outcomes. The assumption that staff are continually engaged in a calculated pursuit of their own interests underestimates the capacity of teachers to

work in harmony with colleagues for the benefit of their pupils and students. The focus on power as the determinant of outcomes may not be wholly appropriate for a cerebral profession such as teaching. In many situations teachers may well be engaged in genuine debate about the best outcomes for the school rather than evaluating every issue in terms of personal and group advantage. 'The [political] frame is normatively cynical and pessimistic. It overstates the inevitability of conflict and understates the potential for effectiveness and collaboration' (Bolman and Deal, 1984).

4. Political models are regarded primarily as descriptive or explanatory approaches. Their advocates claim that these approaches are realistic portrayals of the decision-making process in schools and colleges. Unlike democratic models, these theories are not intended to be normative or prescriptive. There is no suggestion that teachers *should* pursue their own self-interest simply an assessment, based on observation, that their behaviour is consistent with a political perspective. Nevertheless the less attractive aspects of political models may make them unacceptable to many educationists:

> The amorality that often characterises political perspectives raises questions of values. To what extent does the political perspective, even as it purports to be simply a description of reality, ratify and sanctify some of the least humane and most unsavoury aspects of human systems? (Bolman and Deal, 1984, p. 146)

Despite these weaknesses political models have much to offer to an understanding of schools and colleges. Political theorists rightly draw attention to the significance of groups as a potent influence on policy formulation. The emphasis on conflict may be overdrawn but it is valuable as a counterbalance to the optimistic harmony bias of democratic models. The view that disagreement is likely to be resolved ultimately by the relative power of participants is also a persuasive contribution to our understanding of educational institutions. Political models offer valuable insights into the operation of schools and colleges but, as Baldridge *et al.* (1978, pp. 43–44) demonstrate, they do not provide a complete picture of policy-making in education:

> This political model is not a substitute for the bureaucratic or collegial models of academic decision making. In a very real sense each of those addresses a separate set of problems and they often provide complementary interpretations. The political model also has many strengths,

however, and we offer it as a strong contender for interpreting academic governance.

References

Bacharach, S.B. and Lawler, E.J. (1980) *Power and Politics in Organisations*, Jossey Bass, San Francisco

Baldridge, J.V. (1971) *Power and Conflict in the University*, John Wiley, New York

Baldridge, J.V., Curtis, D.V., Ecker, G. and Riley, G.L. (1978) *Policy Making and Effective Leadership*, Jossey Bass, San Francisco

Becher, T. and Kogan, M. (1980) *Process and Structure in Higher Education*, Gower, Aldershot

Blau, P.M. (1964) *Exchange and Power in Social Life*, John Wiley, New York

Bolman, L.G. and Deal, T.E. (1984) *Modern Approaches to Understanding and Managing Organisations*, Jossey Bass, San Francisco

Clark, B.R. (1983) The Contradictions of Change in Academic Systems, *Higher Education*, Vol. 12, pp 101–116

Cuthbert, R. (1984) *The Management Process*, E324 Management in Post Compulsory Education, Block 3, Part 2, Open University Press, Milton Keynes

Cyert, R.M. (1975) *The Management of Non Profit Organisations*, Lexington, Massachusetts, Lexington Books

Davies, J.L. and Morgan, A.W. (1983) Management of higher education in a period of contraction and uncertainty. In O. Boyd-Barrett, T. Bush, J. Goodey, I. McNay and M. Preedy (Eds.) *Approaches to Post School Management*, Harper and Row, London

Ebbutt, K. and Brown, R. (1978) The structure of power in the F.E. college, *Journal of Further and Higher Education*, (NATFHE) Vol. 2, No. 3, pp. 3–17

Etzioni, A. (1961) *A Comparative Analysis of Complex Organisations*, Free Press, a division of Macmillan Inc., New York

Glatter, R. (1982) The micropolitics of education: issues for training, *Educational Management and Administration*, Vol. 10, No. 2, pp. 160–165

Homans, G.C. (1958) Social behaviour as exchange, *American Journal of Sociology*, Vol. 63, No. 6, pp. 597–606

Homans, G.C. (1974) *Social Behaviour: Its Elementary Forms*, Harcourt Brace Jovanovich, New York

Hoyle, E. (1981) *The Process of Management*, E323 Management and the School, Block 3, Part 1, Open University Press, Milton Keynes

Hoyle, E. (1982) Micropolitics of educational organisations, *Educational Management and Administration*, Vol. 10, No. 2, pp. 87–98

Lortie, D.C. (1969) The balance of control and autonomy in elementary school teaching. In A. Etzioni (Ed.) *The Semi-Professions and Their Organisation*, Free Press, a division of Macmillan Inc., New York

Mackenzie, W.J.M. (1967) *Politics and Social Science*, Penguin, London

Mangham, I. (1979) *The Politics of Organisational Change*, Associated Business Press, Ludgate House, Fleet Street, London

Marland, M. (1982) The politics of improvement in schools, *Educational Management and Administration*, Vol. 10, No. 2, pp. 119–134

Sergiovanni, T.J. (1984) Cultural and competing perspectives in administrative theory and practice. In T.J. Sergiovanni and J.E. Corbally, *Leadership and Organisational Culture*, University of Illinois Press, Chicago

CHAPTER 6

SUBJECTIVE MODELS

Central features of subjective models

Subjective models incorporate those approaches which focus on individuals within organizations rather than the total institution or its subunits. The individual member of an organization is placed at the centre in this group of models, which includes phenomenological and interactionist approaches. These perspectives suggest that each individual has a subjective and selective perception of the organization. Events and situations have different meanings for the various participants in institutions. Organizations are regarded as complex notions which reflect the numerous meanings and perceptions of all the people within them. Organizations are social constructions in the sense that they emerge from the interaction of their participants. They are manifestations of the values and beliefs of individuals rather than the concrete realities presented in formal models. The definition suggested below captures the main elements of these approaches:

> Subjective models assume that organizations are the creations of the people within them. Participants are thought to interpret situations in different ways and these individual perceptions are derived from their background and values. Organizations have different meanings for each of their members and exist only in the experience of those members.

Subjective models became prominent in educational management as a result of the work of Thomas Greenfield in the 1970s. Greenfield is concerned about several aspects of systems theory which he regards as the dominant model of educational organizations. He argues that systems theory is 'bad theory' and criticizes its focus on the institution as a concrete reality:

> Most theories of organisation grossly simplify the nature of the reality with which they deal. The drive to see the organisation as a single kind of entity with a life of its own apart from the perceptions and beliefs of those involved in it blinds us to its complexity and the variety of organisations people create around themselves. (Greenfield, 1973, p. 571)

Greenfield is closely associated with the application of subjective theories to schools and colleges and much of the theory development has come from him, or from others stimulated or provoked by his work.

Subjective models have the following major features:

1. They tend to focus on the beliefs and perceptions of *individual* members of organizations rather than the institutional level or interest groups. While formal and democratic models stress the total institution and political models emphasize subgroups the primacy of individual wishes is at the centre of subjective or phenomenological approaches:

> Phenomenology then seeks to understand as far as we can understand by putting the individual at the centre of the stage where [. . .] other approaches tend to see the individual as one of a collectivity to which the individual generally conforms. (Bruce, 1977, pp. 115–116)

Within schools and colleges, subjective theorists point to the different values and aspirations of individual teachers, non teaching staff and pupils. They all experience the institution from different standpoints and interpret events and situations according to their own background and motivations. Ribbins *et al.* (1981, p. 170) argue:

> [. . .] the school is not the same reality for all its teachers. Each teacher brings a perspective to the school, and to his place within it, which is to some extent unique. There are [. . .] as many realities as there are teachers.

2. Subjective models are concerned with the *meanings* placed on events by the individual members of organizations. The focus is on the individual interpretation of behaviour rather than the situations and actions themselves. According to Greenfield (1975), 'organisations are to be understood in terms of people's beliefs about their behaviour within them' rather than on the basis of external observations of that behaviour. It is assumed that individuals may have different interpretations of the same event, as Silverman (1970, p. 130) suggests:

People assign meanings to situations and to the actions of others and react in terms of the interpretation suggested by these meanings [. . .] The same individual even may, at different times or in different situations, assign varying meanings to what appears to an observer to be the same act.

In schools there may be differences of interpretation between the head and other staff who often derive divergent meanings from the same event. Hoyle (1981, p. 45) draws attention to one familiar example of such discrepancies:

When a head talks about his school on public occasions teachers often remark that they do not recognise the place, and, because this view of reality is different from that of the head's they may assume that he is deliberately misleading. But a phenomenological view would hold that we have here *competing* realities, the head and the teachers see the world differently with each perspective having its own legitimacy.

3. The different meanings placed on situations by the various participants are products of their *background, experience and values*. So the interpretation of events depends on the beliefs held by each member of the organization. Greenfield (1979, p. 103) asserts that formal theories make the mistake of treating the meanings of leaders as if they were the objective realities of the organization:

[. . .] life in organisations is filled with contending ideologies [. . .] Too frequently in the past, organisation and administrative theory has [. . .] taken sides in the ideological battles of social process and presented as 'theory' the views of a dominating set of values, the views of rulers, elites, and their administrators.

One possible outcome of the different meanings placed on events may be conflict between participants. Where there are 'competing systems of interpretation' (Silverman, 1970) subjective models may take on some of the characteristics of political theories. Individuals may come together in groups where meanings coincide and engage in political behaviour in pursuit of objectives. However, conflict is only one of several possible outcomes and should not be regarded as a norm. Rather the assumption is that meanings are highly personal, often subtle, and subject to a myriad of influences.

4. Subjective models treat *structure* as essentially a product of human interaction rather than something which is fixed or predetermined. The organization charts which are characteristic of formal models (see Chapter 3) are regarded as fictions in that they cannot predict the behaviour of

individuals. Subjective theorists reject the view that people have to conform to the structure of organizations.

> Most managers appear to be of the opinion that structure in organisations is pre-existent, that all organisations have a predetermined structure into which people must fit. This is not so. Structure is simply a description of what people do and how they relate; organisation structure is a grossly simplified description of jobs and relationships. [. . .] A structure cannot be imposed on an organisation, it can only derive from what people do. (Gray, 1982)

Subjective approaches move the emphasis away from structure towards a consideration of behaviour and process. Individual behaviour is thought to reflect the personal qualities and aspirations of the participants rather than the formal roles they occupy. The variable nature of human behaviour means that organizations are subject to change, as Greenfield (1980, p. 40) claims:

> There is no ultimate reality about organisations, only a state of constant flux. Organisations are at once both the products of action and its cause. We act out of past circumstances and drive towards those we intend for the future. Social realities are constantly created and re-shaped.

Subjective theorists are particularly critical of those approaches which attribute 'human' characteristics to organizations or regard structure as something independent of its members. Silverman (1970, p. 134) comments on this tendency to reify organizations:

> The existence of society depends upon it being continuously confirmed in the actions of its members. [. . .] We reify society if we regard it as having an existence which is separate from and above the actions of men.

5. Subjective approaches emphasize the significance of individual purposes and deny the existence of organizational *goals*. 'What is an organisation that it can have such a thing as a goal?', asks Greenfield (1973). The view that organizations have no existence independent of their members leads on naturally to the assumption that individuals, and not organizations, have objectives. The portrayal of organizations as powerful goal-seeking entities is treated with disdain:

> In subjective theory, because organisations have no corporeal existence apart from the experience members have of them, there can be no 'objectives' for an organisation only objectives for individual members. Furthermore, the nature of organisations as associations of people means that they are at best means to an end; that is they serve purposes. The purposes, however, are

individual purposes – whatever members require the organisation to do in order that something or other may be achieved. (Gray, 1982).

Applying the subjective model – Rivendell School

The essence of subjective approaches is the view that the individual participant is at the heart of organizations and should not be regarded as simply a cog within the institution. The meanings placed on events by their members are thought to be central to our understanding of schools and colleges. Analysis of educational institutions thus requires a subjective dimension if a complete picture is to emerge. However, there are very few empirical studies of schools or colleges which adopt a subjective or phenomenological perspective. One significant exception is the study of pastoral care at 'Rivendell' school (Best *et al.*, 1979, 1983; Ribbins *et al.*, 1981).

In their two-year study of Rivendell, Best and his colleagues give explicit recognition to the value of subjective approaches while acknowledging the methodological difficulties they pose:

> We accept the force of the argument that to explain any social phenomenon it is necessary to establish the subjective meanings which relevant actors attach to that phenomenon, but it is difficult to see how one can establish *meanings* in any hard and fast way. Meanings are not directly observable in the world like physical objects are, and it would be folly indeed to imagine that imputing meanings to actors or situations was something the researcher could lightly undertake. (Best *et al.*, 1983, p. 58)

The researchers adopted several approaches to ascertain the meanings placed on events by staff at Rivendell. There were interviews with fifty-nine of the eighty-two staff, supported by observation of teachers in various situations. Any discrepancies between the accounts of different staff, or inconsistencies between teachers' comments and their behaviour, were taken up at subsequent interviews. 'In this way, we were able to reach a position in which we are fairly confident of the validity of the interpretations we finally made' (Best *et al.*, 1983).

The authors' interpretation of the stated views and behaviour of Rivendell's teachers depended on the context of the statement or action. The implication of the study is that staff may modify their opinions according to the occasion and the nature of the audience. This variation in the manifest positions of teachers makes it difficult to ascertain their real feelings about situations and events:

> [. . .] what a teacher *says* has to be interpreted in the light of the *context* in

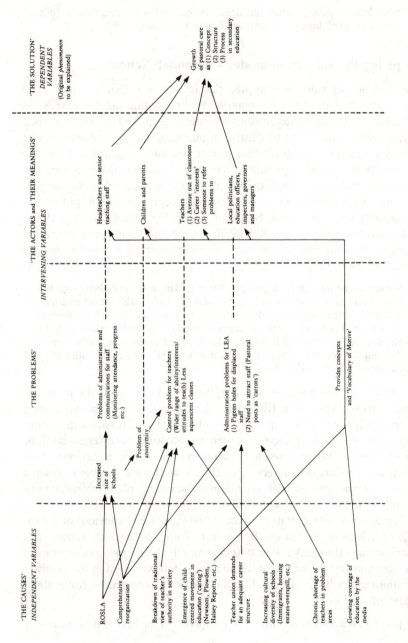

Figure 6.1 A subjective model of pastoral care (from Best *et al.* 1979)

'THE CAUSES'
INDEPENDENT VARIABLES

'THE PROBLEMS'

'THE ACTORS and THEIR MEANINGS'
INTERVENING VARIABLES

'THE SOLUTION'
DEPENDENT VARIABLES
(Original *phenomenon* to be explained)

ROSLA

Comprehensive reorganization

Breakdown of traditional view of teacher's authority in society

Emergence of child-centred movement in education ('caring') (Newsom, Plowden, Halsey Reports, etc.)

Teacher union demands for an adequate career structure

Increasing cultural diversity of schools (Immigrants, housing estates-overspill, etc.)

Chronic shortage of teachers in problem areas

Growing coverage of education by the media

Increased size of schools

Problems of administration and communications for staff (Monitoring attendance, progress, etc.)

Problem of anonymity

Control problem for teachers (Wider range of ability/interests/attitudes to teach) Less aquiescent classes

Administration problems for LEA
(1) Pigeon holes for displaced staff
(2) Need to attract staff (Pastoral posts as 'carrots')

Provides concepts and 'Vocabulary of Motive'

Headteachers and senior teaching staff

Children and parents

Teachers
(1) Avenue out of classroom
(2) Career 'interests'
(3) Someone to refer problems to

Local politicians, education officers, inspectors, governors and managers

Growth of pastoral care as (1) Concept (2) Structure (3) Process in secondary education

which he says it [. . .] Although at Rivendell many senior staff spoke warmly and supportively of the school's pastoral care arrangements at meetings of feeder school parents, this was not necessarily the case at other times. In the context of interviews and informal discussions with researchers, some of these teachers showed themselves capable of a criticism of the school's pastoral arrangements to which their statements in more public situations gave no clue. (Ribbins *et al.*, 1981, pp. 162–163)

Best and his colleagues were concerned to test the 'conventional wisdom' that teachers have the interests of the children at the centre of their approach to pastoral care. Their hypothesis was that there may be significant differences between the public statements and the reality of pastoral care in schools. The authors' approach to this apparent contradiction was to focus on the subjective interpretations of staff rather than the official version of pastoral care policy.

In developing an analytical theory of the growth of institutional pastoral care, we have given great weight to the actors and their perceptions of the 'problem' to which pastoral care is intended to provide the solution. Their perceptions will [. . .] be influenced by their own interests. [. . .] The naive assumption that pastoral care systems deal only with the problems of the children pre-empts a consideration of the possibility that the creation of pastoral care systems and their posts of responsibility may have been a response to problems confronting teachers, headteachers, LEAs and educational administrators. (Best *et al.*, 1979, pp. 36/38)

The authors identify a number of variables which may have contributed to the growth of pastoral care concepts and structures in schools. These include comprehensive reorganization, the raising of the school leaving age and the demands for an adequate career structure, particularly for non-graduates from former secondary modern schools. All those individuals with an interest in the school apply their own interpretations to events and problems and necessarily influence the development of pastoral care and guidance in schools.

Figure 6.1 illustrates the relationships between the factors which influenced the development of pastoral care and the subjective meanings of participants. The independent variables led to a number of perceived problems including communication and control in larger schools and staffing difficulties arising from reorganization. Actors inside and outside the school provided their own interpretations of these developments and their meanings eventually coalesced in the growth of pastoral care concepts, structures and processes.

The public statements about pastoral care at Rivendell reflect the conventional wisdom of a child-centred approach. Staff have an obvious interest in maintaining and enhancing the reputation of their school and official pastoral care policy has to be interpreted in that light:

> Headteachers and senior staff have a vested interest in portraying their school as a 'caring' institution because their own public image, and therefore to some extent their *self* image, depends in no small measure on the evaluation which the public at large make of the institution for which they are responsible. This is heightened when a school is in the position of Rivendell Comprehensive, battling constantly against what staff believed to be an unjustifiably poor reputation in the local community. (Best *et al.*, 1983, p. 57)

An example of the discontinuity between the school's official policy and pastoral care practice occurred during the research period at Rivendell. Ribbins *et al.* (1981, p. 166) record a significant incident which serves to highlight this contrast:

> [. . .] we once interviewed a fairly senior member of staff who spent some time telling us how much he cared for children and how the 'interests' of his pupils came first with him. At this point a lower school boy knocked, and without waiting for permission, entered the room. He was immediately subjected to a diatribe of impressive proportions and sent from the room to 'wait to be dealt with later'. Once the boy had left, the teacher took up his account exactly where he had left it before the interruption, but to two researchers who were now a good deal more sceptical than they had been a few minutes before.

The numerous perceptions which emerged from the many interviews and observations at Rivendell were classified by the authors into five perspectives on pastoral care. These perspectives represent clusters of the various interpretations of school policy suggested by the staff. The five approaches are illustrated by extracts from the researchers' field notes and interview transcripts:

The *child-centred* perspective focuses on the problems of the child as an individual. It centres on issues of personal happiness and adaptation and supports the conventional wisdom of the school as a caring environment for its pupils. One teacher gave the following example of a pastoral care problem which the authors classified as 'child-centred'.

> I have a girl who was a battered baby [. . .] she is very much a 'loner'. She had a bowel problem as well which makes her unpopular with the other children [. . .] every time she had a PE period she would run away. When I asked her why, all she would say was 'I hate this school'. I got some of the girls together and talked about how we needed to convince her that we liked her. The girls

cooperated in this. Now she doesn't run away. [. . .] Now she thinks she likes the school. (Best *et al.*, 1983, p. 65).

In this case the teacher interpreted the situation as a problem of personal happiness and adaptation rather than a disciplinary problem. The solution adopted by the teacher was essentially child centred and involved an interpersonal strategy which appeared to be successful.

The *pupil-centred* perspective relates primarily to children in their academic roles as pupils. The pastoral provision in the school is evaluated in terms of its function as a facilitator of a pupil's academic performance, as one teacher's comment suggests: 'What you have to do is to try to get to a position where the child can do his best work [. . .] To get the best work you must care for the child' (Best *et al.*, 1983). Here the concern for pupils' welfare is mainly geared to the promotion of their learning rather than the personal happiness of the children as individuals.

The *discipline-centred* perspective focuses on problems of teachers' control in the classroom and the difficulties created by the failure of other staff to give them the necessary backing. Here the school's pastoral care provision is perceived as the vehicle for the control of pupils. One form tutor, when asked about her role, responded in part by emphasizing the importance of discipline:

[. . .] there are school problems, for example, if they are in trouble with another teacher. If it comes to my attention I say 'I don't want children in my class to be in trouble'. If they get into trouble I tell them I will do something about it; that is, not only will the teacher punish them but I will punish them as well. (Best *et al.*, 1983, p. 71)

For certain teachers the pastoral care structure of the school was assessed in terms of discipline and control. Pastoral staff were there to be 'used' by teachers to resolve their problems of control. Rivendell has both a house system and a year structure and one tutor was asked to distinguish between the vertical and horizontal structures. His response fits the discipline centred approach to pastoral care:

As far as I can see, there is little in the way of distinguishing features between them. In individual cases the Head of House may be stronger than the Head of Year, so you go to the former. At least this arrangement gives you two bites at the cherry: if one doesn't pay off the other does. (Best *et al.*, 1983, p. 72)

The *administrator-centred* perspective relates to the efficiency of the school as an administrative organization. At Rivendell the dual structure of years and houses was criticized by several staff on the grounds of organizational complexity. One senior teacher thought that there was:

> [. . .] too much duplication. I just think it is sloppy, quite frankly [. . .] It should not be necessary to have more than twenty people in positions of authority, and in some schools it is starting to look like everyone is. (Best et al., 1983, p. 76)

A similar view was expressed by a junior member of staff:

> At the moment there are too many people; for example, a fifth-form tutor may have to contact Farley as Head of Humanities, Bailey as Head of Year, and Austen as Head of House, on a problem that a child has in Humanities. [. . .] This is an instance of increasing bureaucracy in schools. (Best et al., 1983, p. 77)

Teachers who adopt an administrator-centred approach thus evaluate pastoral structures in terms of their administrative efficiency rather than their effectiveness as welfare systems.

The *subject-centred* perspective relates primarily to the academic role of the teacher. Staff are concerned largely with their work as subject specialists and have little regard to their pastoral responsibilities. The learning situation is perceived as one where distinct subjects are taught by specialists. Best et al. (1983, p. 78) describe the attitude adopted by one teacher at Rivendell:

> One teacher [. . .] stood out from the rest because of her tendency to emphasise her role as the teacher of a *subject* rather than as a teacher of pupils or a 'carer' for children. The pastoral arrangements of the school did not seem to hold any importance for her, and she was simply uninterested in her own pastoral role as a form tutor.

The five perspectives identified by the authors are conceptually distinct but few teachers fit neatly into a single category. Nevertheless, the classification provides a useful framework of analysis for pastoral care while serving as a valuable illustration of the subjective model. The study confirms the view of subjective theorists that the school is not a monolithic organization. Rather each teacher has an individual interpretation of the school and these meanings may cluster into broad perspectives as was the case at Rivendell.

Subjective models: goals, structure, environment and leadership

Subjective models differ from other approaches in that they stress the *goals* of individuals rather than the objectives of the institution or its subunits.

Members of organizations are thought to have their own personal aims which they seek to achieve within the institution. The notion of organizational objectives, central to formal and democratic models, is rejected, as Coulson (1985, p. 44) suggests:

> [. . .] it is not schools or organisations but people who pursue goals or aims. [. . .] Teachers, especially perhaps headteachers, hold and pursue their own personal goals within schools, and many of these may be only tenuously linked to the teaching-learning process. [. . .] These individual goals relate to the person's self-esteem, career advancement, and job satisfaction.

Individual goals, then, may be related only tangentially to the organization. Often they are not concerned with wider institutional issues but rather reflect the personal wishes of the staff as individuals. Greenfield (1973, p. 568) argues:

> [. . .] many people do not hold goals [. . .] in the sense of *ends* that the organisation is to accomplish, but merely hold a set of beliefs about what it is *right* to do in an organisation.

The denial of the concept of organizational objectives creates difficulties because most teachers are aware of the purposes and aims of schools and colleges. Many staff would acknowledge the existence of goals such as teaching all children to read or achieving a good record in public examinations. At a commonsense level these are regarded as organizational objectives. Greenfield (1973, p. 557) suggests that goals which appear to be those of the organization are really the objectives of powerful individuals within the institution. He claims that 'the goals of the organisation are the current preoccupations and intentions of the dominant organisational coalition'. In schools it is assumed that headteachers may possess sufficient power to promote their own purposes as the objectives of the institution. In this view, organizational goals are a chimera; they are simply the personal aims of the most powerful individuals.

Subjective models regard organizational *structure* as an outcome of the interaction of participants rather than a fixed entity which is independent of the people within the institution. Structure, then, is a product of the behaviour of individuals and serves to explain the relationships between members of organizations. Cuthbert (1984, p. 60) suggests:

> [. . .] an organisation structure should be seen as something constructed and sustained through human interaction [. . .] Structure is a description of behaviour rather than a constraint upon it; structure describes what people do and how they relate.

Formal and democratic models tend to regard structure as a fixed and stable aspect of organizations while subjective approaches emphasize the different meanings placed on structure by the individuals within the institution. The management team might be portrayed as a participative forum by the headteacher but regarded as a vehicle for the one-way dissemination of information by other staff. Teachers interpret relationships in schools and colleges in different ways and, in doing so, they influence the structures within their institutions. However, there are variations in the amount of power which individuals can wield in seeking to modify structure, as Ranson *et al.* (1980, p. 7) explain:

> Organisational structures are shaped and constituted by members' provinces of meaning, by their deep-seated interpretive schemes, and by the surface articulation of values and interests. More accurately, however, structuring is typically the privilege of *some* organizational actors [. . .] The analytical focus then becomes the relations of power which enable some organisational members to constitute and re-create organisational structures according to their provinces of meaning.

In education, heads and principals are often able to impose their interpretations of structure on the institutions they lead. They can introduce a faculty structure to promote interdepartmental cooperation, for example, but the effectiveness of such a change depends crucially on the attitudes of the staff concerned. Structural change alone may be ineffective if it lacks the support of the people within the organization, as Greenfield (1973, p. 565) demonstrates:

> Shifting the external trappings of organisation, which we may call organisation structure if we wish, turns out to be easier than altering the deeper meanings and purposes which people express through organisation [. . .] we are forced to see problems of organisational structure as inherent not in 'structure' itself but in the human meanings and purposes which support that structure. Thus it appears that we cannot solve organisational problems by either abolishing or improving structure alone; we must also look at their human foundations.

While accepting the strictures of Greenfield about the limitations of structural change there are obvious difficulties in understanding and responding to the various personal interpretations of situations in organizations. The elusive and variable nature of human meanings suggests that organizational change may be a slow and uncertain process if it depends primarily on an understanding of individual wishes and beliefs.

In subjective models little attention is paid to relationships between organizations and their *environment*. This may be because organizations are not portrayed as viable entities. The focus is on the meanings placed on events by people within the organization rather than interaction between the institution and groups or individuals external to it. The notion of outside bodies exerting influence on the school or college makes little sense when subjective models claim that organizations have no existence independent of the individuals within them.

Where subjective models deal with the environment at all the emphasis is on links between individuals and external influences rather than outside pressures on the total institution. The assumption that human behaviour stems from a personal interpretation of events raises the issue of the source of these meanings. Some theorists suggest that these meanings emanate from the wider society. Silverman (1970), for example, considers that 'the environment in which an organisation is located might usefully be regarded as a source of meanings through which members defined their actions and made sense of the actions of others'. Greenfield (1973, p. 558) adopts a similar approach, claiming that 'the kinds of organisation we live in derive not from their structure but from attitudes and experiences we bring to organisations from the wider society in which we live'.

In education the interpretations of individuals may originate from several sources. For teachers a major influence is the professional socialization that results from their training and the early years of teaching. In addition several key individuals outside the institution emanate from the same professional background. These include HM Inspectorate and local advisers and education officers. These professional influences tend to produce shared meanings and values. A stronger view is suggested by Watkins (1983) who claims that professionalism is a covert method of control, ensuring that teachers accept the authority of heads and other senior professionals.

Teachers are also subject to a wider range of influences such as their family, friends and members of clubs and societies external to the school. These sources may lead to a diversity of meanings. Greenfield (1973, p. 559) prefers to emphasize differences in interpretation rather than shared meanings.

> This notion of organisations as dependent upon meanings and purposes which individuals bring to organisations from the wider society does not require that all individuals share the same meanings and purposes. On the contrary, the views I am outlining here should make us seek to discover the varying meanings and objectives that individuals bring to the organisations of which they are a part.

The concept of *leadership* fits rather uneasily within the framework of subjective models. Individuals place different meanings on events and this applies to all members, whatever their formal position in the organization. People who occupy leadership roles have their own values and beliefs and it is assumed that they have their own goals in the same way as other participants. Management can be regarded, then, as the pursuit of their own interests by individual leaders. A key difference between managers and other members of organizations is that the former may be in a position to impose their interpretations of events on the latter. Management may be seen as a form of control with heads and principals elevating their meanings to the status of school or college policy. These leaders may use their resources of power to require compliance with these interpretations even where other staff do not share those meanings.

Subjective theorists prefer to stress the personal qualities of individuals rather than the formally ascribed positions in the organization. As Gray (1982) suggests, 'situations require appropriate behaviours for their resolution and this can only be done by those best fitted to deal with them irrespective of their formal position or status in the organisation'. This emphasis on the personal attributes of staff leads on to the view that formal roles are an inadequate guide to behaviour. Rather individuals bring their own values and meanings to their work, as Gray (1979, p. 126) demonstrates:

> I do not find it satisfactory to describe organisations solely in terms of position, roles and prescribed role behaviour. Different personalities will behave quite differently in similar circumstances and however strong structural pressures may be, the results may not be at all similar for two different personalities.

The limitations of subjective models

Subjective models are primarily prescriptive approaches in that they reflect beliefs about the nature of organizations rather than presenting a clear framework for analysis. Their protagonists make several cogent points about educational institutions but this alternative perspective does not represent a comprehensive approach to the management of schools and colleges. Subjective models can be regarded as 'anti theories' in that they emerged as a reaction to the perceived weaknesses of the formal models. Greenfield is particularly zealous in his advocacy of subjective approaches and his rejection of many of the central assumptions of conventional organizational theory.

The subjective perspective does offer some valuable insights which act as a corrective to the more rigid features of formal models. The focus on individual interpretations of events is a useful antidote to the uniformity of systems and structural theories. Likewise the substitution of individual aims for organizational objectives is an important contribution to our understanding of schools and colleges. However, subjective models have four significant weaknesses which serve to limit their validity.

1. Subjective models are *strongly normative* in that they reflect the attitudes and beliefs of their supporters. Greenfield, in particular, has faced a barrage of criticism, much of it fuelled by emotion rather than reason, for his advocacy of phenomenological approaches to organizations. Willower (1980, p. 7), for example, claims that subjective models are 'ideological' and attacks their supporters:

> [Phenomenological] perspectives feature major ideological components and their partisans tend to be true believers when promulgating their positions rather than offering them for critical examination and test. [. . .] they can be found in much phenomenologically oriented writing, now even in organisation theory and educational administration where the message is being preached by recent converts who previously must have been unaware of the phenomenological perspective, or perhaps had just not thought much about it, but now embrace it wholeheartedly and with the dedication of the convert.

Comments such as these generate more heat than light but serve to illustrate the intensity of feeling engendered by Greenfield's challenge to conventional theory. Nevertheless, there is substance in Willower's criticism of phenomenological perspectives. Subjective models comprise a series of principles which have attracted the committed support of a few adherents, notably Greenfield. These principles do not comprise a coherent body of theory. The focus on individual meanings offers an additional dimension in our attempts to understand schools and colleges but, on its own, subjective theory fails to explain processes and behaviour in education.

2. Subjective models seem to assume the existence of an organization within which individual behaviour and interpretation occur. However, there is no clear indication of the nature of the organization. It is acknowledged that teachers work within a school or college but these bodies are not recognized as viable entities. Educational institutions are thought to have no structure beyond that created by their members. Schools and colleges are not regarded as having objectives because only people can have goals. So organizations are nothing more than the product of the meanings of their

participants. In emphasizing the interpretations of individuals subjective theorists neglect the institutions within which individuals behave, interact and derive meanings. Silverman (1970) asserts that 'the action approach tends to assume an existing system in which action occurs but cannot successfully explain the nature of the system'. Subjective theorists are open to the charge that they have undermined conventional organizational theory but have failed to produce a viable alternative.

3. Subjective theorists imply that meanings are so individual that there may be as many interpretations as people. In practice, though, these meanings tend to cluster into patterns which do enable participants and observers to make valid generalizations about organizations. The idea of totally independent perceptions is suspect because individual meanings depend on participants' background and experience. Teachers, for example, emanate from a common professional background which often results in shared meanings and purposes. Hoyle (1976, p. 4) is critical of Greenfield's stance on this issue:

> The major criticism of the system approach is that it gives ontological priority to the abstract properties of organisations over the actions of those who 'people' them at any given time. It is true that some system approaches [. . .] have reified the organisation but it is an excess of a different kind to claim that the organisation is *nothing more* than how groups of participants define it, and that there are as many organisations as there are definitions.

Subjective models also fail to explain the many similarities between schools. If individual perceptions provide the only valid definitions of organizations how is it that educational institutions have so many common features? A teacher from one school would find some unique qualities in other schools but would also come across many familiar characteristics. This suggests that there is an entity called a 'school' which may evoke similar impressions among participants and observers alike. Hills (1980, p. 35) argues that much behaviour in educational institutions is unsurprising:

> [. . .] one of the most noteworthy features of the settings we term organisations (schools, hospitals, firms, universities and so forth) is that they are characterised by a high degree of order. One may have great difficulty in making refined predictions about the details of what goes on in such settings, but one rarely finds conditions so altered that he cannot recognise where he is.

4. A major criticism of subjective models is that they provide no guidelines for managerial action. Leaders are left with nothing more substantial than the need to acknowledge the individual meanings placed on

events by members of organizations. Formal models stress the authority of heads to make decisions while pointing to the need to acknowledge the place of official bodies such as management teams and academic boards. Democratic models emphasize the desirability of reaching agreement with colleagues and providing opportunities for participation in decision-making. Political models accentuate the significance of building coalitions among interest groups in order to ensure support for policy proposals. Subjective models offer no such formula for the development of leadership strategies. As Greenfield (1980) himself acknowledges, 'this conception of organisations does not make them easy to control or to change'.

Despite these limitations the subjective model has introduced some important considerations into the debate on the nature of schools and colleges. The emphasis on the primacy of individual meanings is a valuable aid to our understanding of educational institutions. A recognition of the different values and motivations of the people who work in organizations is an essential element if they are to be managed successfully. Certainly teachers are not simply automatons carrying out routine activities with mechanical precision. Rather they deploy their individual skills and talents in the conduct of their work with pupils. 'Few of us can see ourselves as smoothly functioning components of a vast machine' (Theodossin, 1983).

Subjective models provide an important new slant on organizations but the perspective is *partial*. The stress on individual interpretation of events is valid but ultimately it leads to a blind alley. If there are as many meanings as teachers, as Greenfield claims, our capacity to understand educational institutions is likely to be fully stretched. If individual meanings are themselves subject to variation according to the context, as Best *et al.* (1983) suggest, then the number of permutations is likely to be overwhelming. In practice interpretations do cluster into patterns if only because shared meanings emerge from the professional socialization undergone by teachers during training and probation. If there are common meanings then it is possible to derive some generalizations about behaviour. Best *et al.* (1983) adopted a subjective approach in their study of 'Rivendell' but they were able to identify five distinct perspectives on pastoral care arising from the individual interpretations of teaching staff.

One way of understanding the relationship between formal and subjective models may be in terms of scale. Some writers argue that formal models are particularly helpful in understanding the total institution and relationships between the organization and elements in its structure. In education the interaction between departments or pastoral groups and the institutional level may be explained best by using bureaucratic and structural concepts. However, subjective approaches may be especially valid in examining individual behaviour and relationships between individuals. Theodossin (1983, p. 83) suggests:

> [. . .] the systems approach may be likened to a kind of aerial photograph which seeks to provide a broad overview; and the phenomenological approach to a variety of microscopic photographs in which detail is enlarged to aid perception.

Formal and subjective models thus provide complementary approaches to our understanding of organizations. The formal structure of schools and colleges should be examined alongside consideration of the individual attitudes and perceptions of staff and pupils. Just as institutions cannot be understood without a consideration of the meanings of participants so these interpretations are of limited value unless the more formal and stable aspects of organizations are also examined.

References

Best, R.E., Ribbins, P.M. and Jarvis, C.B. (1979) Pastoral care: reflections on a research strategy, *British Educational Research Journal*, Vol. 5, No. 1, pp. 35–43

Best, R., Ribbins, P., Jarvis, C. and Oddy, D. (1983) *Education and Care*, Heinemann, London

Bruce, D. (1977) The phenomenology debate, *Educational Administration*, Vol. 6, No. 1, pp. 114–117

Coulson, A. (1985) *The Managerial Behaviour of Primary School Heads*, Collected Original Resources in Education, Carfax Publishing Company, Abingdon

Cuthbert, R. (1984) *The Management Process*, E323 Management in Post Compulsory Education, Block 3, Part 2, Open University Press, Milton Keynes

Gray, H. (1979) Personal viewpoint: organisations as subjectivities, *Educational Administration*, Vol. 7, No. 2, pp 122–129

Gray, H.L. (1982) A perspective on organisation theory. In H.L. Gray (Ed.) *The Management of Educational Institutions*, Falmer Press, Lewes

Greenfield, T.B. (1973) Organisations as social inventions: rethinking assumptions about change, *Journal of Applied Behavioural Science*, Vol. 9, No. 5, pp 551–574

Greenfield, T.B. (1975) Theory about organisations: a new perspective and its implications for schools. In M. Hughes (Ed.) *Administering Education: International Challenge*, Athlone Press, London

Greenfield, T.B. (1979) Organisation theory as ideology, *Curriculum Enquiry*, Vol. 9, No. 2, pp 97–112

Greenfield, T.B. (1980) The man who comes back through the door in the wall: discovering truth, discovering self, discovering organisations, *Educational Administration Quarterly*, Vol. 16, No. 3, pp 26–59

Hills, R.J. (1980) A critique of Greenfield's 'New Perspective', *Educational Administration Quarterly*, Vol. 16, No. 1, pp 20–44

Hoyle, E. (1976) Barr Greenfield and organisational theory: a symposium, *Educational Administration*, Vol. 5, No. 1, pp 4–6

Hoyle, E. (1981) *The Process of Management*, E323 Management and the School, Block 3, Part 1, Open University Press, Milton Keynes

Ranson, S., Hinings, B. and Greenwood, R. (1980) The structuring of organisational structures, *Administrative Science Quarterly*, Vol. 25, No. 1, 1–17

Ribbins, P.M., Jarvis, C.B., Best, R.E. and Oddy, D.M. (1981) Meanings and contexts: the problem of interpretation in the study of a school, *Research in Educational Management and Administration*, British Educational Management and Administration Society, Birmingham

Silverman, D. (1970) *The Theory of Organisations*, Heinemann, London

Theodossin, E. (1983) Theoretical perspectives on the management of planned educational change, *British Educational Research Journal*, Vol. 9, No. 1, pp 81–90

Watkins, P. (1983) *Class, Control and Contestation in Educational Organisations*, Deakin University, Victoria, Australia

Willower, D.J. (1980) Contemporary issues in theory in educational administration, *Educational Administration Quarterly*, Vol. 16, No. 3, pp 1–25

CHAPTER 7

AMBIGUITY MODELS

Central features of ambiguity models

Ambiguity models include all those approaches which stress uncertainty and unpredictability in organizations. The emphasis is on the instability and complexity of institutional life. These theories suggest that organizational objectives are problematic and that institutions experience difficulty in ordering their priorities. Subunits are portrayed as relatively autonomous groups which are only loosely connected with one another and with the institution itself. Decision-making occurs within formal and informal settings where participation is fluid. Individuals are part-time members of policy-making groups who move in and out of the picture according to the nature of the topic and the interests of the potential participants. Ambiguity is a prevalent feature of complex organizations such as schools and colleges and is likely to be particularly acute during periods of rapid change. The definition indicated below incorporates the main elements of these approaches:

> Ambiguity models assume that turbulence and unpredictability are dominant features of organisations. There is no clarity over the objectives of institutions and their processes are not properly understood. Participation in policy making is fluid as members opt in or out of decision opportunities.

Ambiguity models are associated with a group of mainly American theorists who developed their ideas in the 1970s. They were dissatisfied with the explanations of organizational behaviour furnished by the formal models. These were regarded as inadequate for many organizations and particularly unsuitable during phases of instability. March (1982) points to the jumbled reality in certain kinds of organization:

> Theories of choice underestimate the confusion and complexity surrounding actual decision making. Many things are happening at once; technologies are changing and poorly understood; alliances, preferences, and perceptions are changing; problems, solutions, opportunities, ideas, people, and outcomes are mixed together in a way that makes their interpretation uncertain and their connections unclear.

Unlike many other perspectives, the data supporting ambiguity models have been drawn largely from educational settings. Schools and colleges are characterized as having uncertain goals, unclear technology and fluid participation in decision-making. They are also subject to changing demands from their environments. These factors lead March and Olsen (1976) to assert that 'ambiguity is a major feature of decision making in most public and educational organisations'.

Ambiguity models have the following major features:

1. There is a lack of clarity about the *goals* of the organization. Many institutions are thought to have inconsistent and opaque objectives. Formal models assume that organizations have clear purposes which guide the activities of their members. Ambiguity perspectives, by contrast, suggest that goals are so vague that they can be used to justify almost any behaviour. Indeed it may be that aims become clear only through the behaviour of organizational members, as Cohen and March (1974, p. 3) claim:

> It is difficult to impute a set of goals to the organisation that satisfies the standard consistency requirements of theories of choice. The organisation appears to operate on a variety of inconsistent and ill-defined preferences. It can be described better as a loose collection of changing ideas than as a coherent structure. It discovers preferences through action more often than it acts on the basis of preferences.

Educational institutions are regarded as typical in having no clearly defined objectives. The discretion ascribed to teachers enables them to identify their own educational purposes and to behave in accordance with those purposes for most of their professional activities. Because teachers work independently for much of their time they may experience little difficulty in pursuing their own interests. As a result schools and colleges are thought to have no coherent pattern of objectives:

> [. . .] it is not very clear what the goals of the school are. Different members of the school may perceive different goals or attribute different priorities to the same goals or even be unable to define goals which have any operational

meaning. Thus whilst it is commonly expected that those who work in schools should have some overall purpose it is likely that the organisational context of many schools actually renders this impossible or very difficult. Hence schools face an ambiguity of purpose. (Bell, 1980, p. 188)

2. Ambiguity models assume that organizations have a *problematic technology* in that their processes are not properly understood. Institutions are unclear about how outcomes emerge from their activities. This is particularly true of client serving organizations where the technology is necessarily tailored to the needs of the individual client. In education it is not clear how pupils and students acquire knowledge and skills so the processes of teaching are surrounded by doubt and uncertainty. Bell (1980, p. 188) refers to the prevalence of ambiguity about the central functions of schools:

> [. . .] teachers are often unsure about what it is they want their pupils to learn, about what it is the pupils have learned about and how, if at all, learning has actually taken place. The learning process is inadequately understood and therefore pupils may not always be learning effectively whilst the basic technology available in schools is often not understood because its purposes are only vaguely recognised. [. . .] Since the related technology is so unclear the processes of teaching and learning are clouded in ambiguity.

3. Ambiguity models suggest that organizations are characterized by *fragmentation*. Institutions are broken down into groups which have internal coherence based on common values and goals. Links between the groups are more tenuous and unpredictable. Weick (1976, p. 3) uses the term 'loose coupling' to describe relationships between subunits:

> By loose coupling, the author intends to convey the image that coupled events are responsive, *but* that each event also preserves its own identity and some evidence of its physical or logical separateness. [. . .] their attachment may be circumscribed, infrequent, weak in its mutual effects, unimportant, and/or slow to respond [. . .] Loose coupling also carries connotations of impermanence, dissolvability, and tacitness all of which are potentially crucial properties of the 'glue' that holds organisations together.

The concept of loose coupling was first applied to educational institutions and it is particularly appropriate for organizations whose members have a substantial degree of discretion. Client-serving bodies such as schools and colleges fit this metaphor much better than, say, car assembly plants where operations are regimented and predictable. The degree of integration required in education is markedly less, allowing fragmentation to develop and persist.

4. Within ambiguity models organizational *structure* is regarded as prob-

lematic. There is uncertainty over the relative power of the different parts of the institution. Committees and other formal bodies have rights and responsibilities which overlap with each other and with the authority assigned to individual managers. The effective power of each element within the structure varies with the issue and according to the level of participation of committee members. The more complex the formal structure of the organization the greater the ambiguity. In this view the organization charts discussed in Chapter 3 conceal more than they reveal about the pattern of relationships in institutions.

In education the validity of the formal structure as a representation of the distribution of power depends on the size and complexity of the institution. Many primary schools have a simple authority structure centred on the head and there is little room for misunderstanding. In further and higher education, and in large secondary schools, there is often an elaborate pattern of interlocking committees and working parties. Noble and Pym's (1970, p. 436) assessment of decision-making in a college captures the ambiguity of structure in the larger organizations:

> The lower level officials or committees argue that they, of course, can only make recommendations. Departments must seek the approval of inter-departmental committees, these in turn can only submit reports and recommendations to the general management committee. It is there we are told that decisions must be made [. . .] In the general management committee however, though votes are taken and decisions formally reached, there was a widespread feeling, not infrequently expressed even by some of its senior members, of powerlessness, a feeling that decisions were really taken elsewhere. [. . .] as a committee they could only assent to decisions which had been put up to them from one of the lower tier committees or a sub-committee [. . .]
>
> The common attribution of effective decision making to a higher or lower committee has led the authors to describe the decision-making structure in this organisation as an involuted hierarchy.

5. Ambiguity models tend to be particularly appropriate for *professional client-serving* organizations. In education the pupils and students often demand inputs into the process of decision-making, especially where it has a direct influence on their educational experience. Teachers are expected to be responsive to the perceived needs of their pupils rather than operating under the direct supervision of hierarchical superordinates. The requirement that professionals make individual judgements, and do not necessarily act in accordance with managerial prescriptions, leads on to the view that the larger schools and colleges are correctly portrayed as anarchies:

I believe that large and complex, multipurpose, rapidly expanding or other-wise changing organisations are anarchic [. . .] So are organisations with a high degree of professionalisation among their rank and file; service-producing organisations probably fit this picture better than goods-producing enterprises do. (Enderud, 1980, p. 236)

6. Ambiguity perspectives emphasize that there is *fluid participation* in the management of organizations. Members move in and out of decision-making situations, as Cohen and March (1974, p. 3) suggest:

The participants in the organisation vary among themselves in the amount of time and effort they devote to the organisation; individual participants vary from one time to another. As a result standard theories of power and choice seem to be inadequate.

Bell (1980, p. 189) elaborates on this concept and applies it to the school:

[. . .] the school consists of groups of pupils and teachers all of whom make a wide range of demands on the organisation. By their very nature schools gain and lose large numbers of pupils each year and, until recently, they also experienced a high turnover in teaching staff. [. . .] Membership of the school is also fluid in [. . .] the extent to which individuals are willing and able to participate in its activities. Their degree of commitment may change over time and according to the nature of the activity itself. In this way schools are peopled by participants who wander in and out. The notion of membership is thus ambiguous.

7. A further source of ambiguity is provided by the signals emanating from the organization's *environment*. There is some evidence that education-al institutions are becoming more dependent on elements within their environments. Continuing uncertainties over levels of funding make schools and colleges vulnerable to the vagaries of central and local govern-ment. Parents are able to exercise more power at a time when schools are competing for a diminishing pool of pupils. Many schools are also the beneficiaries of significant financial contributions from parents, who may expect influence commensurate with their levels of spending. Institutions are becoming more open to external groups and, in a period of rapid change, they may experience difficulties in interpreting the various messages being transmitted from the environment. The uncertainty over the significance of external signals adds to the ambiguity of the decision-making process inside the institution.

8. Ambiguity models emphasize that decisions are often *unplanned*. Formal perspectives assume that problems arise, possible solutions are formulated and the most appropriate solution is chosen. The selected

option is then implemented and subject to evaluation in due course. The ambiguity approach claims that this logical sequence rarely occurs in practice. Rather the lack of agreed goals means that decisions have no clear focus. Problems, solutions and participants interact and choices somehow emerge from the confusion. Bell (1980, p. 190) discusses this concept in relation to schools:

> [. . .] the taking of decisions and the solution of the problems cannot be based on some notion of common goals. [. . . they] are more likely to consist of linking together problems, solutions, participants and choices in conditions of ambiguity such that there are no criteria for making the connections. Hence the ideal solution and its related problem may not be linked.

9. Ambiguity models stress the advantages of *decentralization*. Given the complexity and unpredictability of organizations it is suggested that many decisions should be devolved to subunits and individuals. Departments are relatively coherent and may be capable of rapid adaptation to changing circumstances. Subunits may be more sensitive to external pressures and decentralized decision-making avoids the delays and uncertainties associated with the institutional level. Individual and departmental autonomy are seen as appropriate for professional staff who are required to exercise their judgement in dealing with clients. Successful departments are able to expand and thrive while weaker areas may contract or even close during difficult periods. Weick (1976, p. 7) argues that devolution enables organizations to survive while particular subunits are threatened:

> [. . .] if there is a breakdown in one portion of a loosely coupled system then this breakdown is sealed off and does not affect other portions of the organisation [. . .] when any element misfires or decays or deteriorates, the spread of this deterioration is checked in a loosely coupled system [. . .] A loosely coupled system can isolate its trouble spots and prevent the trouble from spreading.

The garbage can model

The most celebrated of the ambiguity perspectives is the garbage can model developed by Cohen and March (1974). The authors conducted research in universities in the USA and concluded that ambiguity is one of the major characteristics of American universities and colleges. They reject the sequential assumptions of the formal models in which decisions are thought to emanate from a rational process. Rather they regard decision-making as fundamentally ambiguous.

A key to understanding the processes within organisations is to view a choice opportunity as a garbage can into which various problems and solutions are dumped by participants. The mix of garbage in a single can depends partly on the labels attached to the alternative cans; but it also depends on what garbage is being produced at the moment, on the mix of cans available, and on the speed with which garbage is collected and removed from the scene. (Cohen and March 1974, p. 81).

The authors focus on four relatively independent streams within organizations. Decisions are outcomes of the interaction of the four streams, identified by Cohen and March (1974, p. 82).

1. *Problems*: Problems are the concern of people inside and outside the organization. They arise over issues of lifestyle; family; frustrations of work; careers; group relations within the organization; distribution of status, jobs, and money; ideology; or current crises of mankind as interpreted by the mass media or the nextdoor neighbor. All require attention. Problems are, however, distinct from choices; and they may not be resolved when choices are made.
2. *Solutions*: A solution is somebody's product. A computer is not just a solution to a problem in payroll management, discovered when needed. It is an answer actively looking for a question. The creation of need is not a curiosity of the market in consumer products; it is a general phenomenon of processes of choice. Despite the dictum that you cannot find the answer until you have formulated the question well, you often do not know what the question is in organizational problem solving until you know the answer.
3. *Participants*: Participants come and go. Since every entrance is an exit somewhere else, the distribution of entrances depends on the attributes of the choice being left as much as it does on the attributes of the new choice. Substantial variation in participation stems from other demands on the participants' time (rather than from features of the decision under study).
4. *Choice opportunities*: These are occasions when an organization is expected to produce behavior that can be called a decision. Opportunities arise regularly, and any organization has ways of declaring an occasion for choice. Contracts must be signed; people hired, promoted, or fired; money spent; and responsibilities allocated.

The authors regard the garbage can model as particularly appropriate for higher education but several of the key ideas are also relevant for schools. The major characteristics of ambiguous goals, unclear technology and fluid participation often apply to secondary schools although they may be less evident in the primary sector.

The garbage can model posits three different ways in which decisions may be made. Only one style applies to any one decision but within a single organization all three styles may be used at different choice opportunities. The authors claim that the decision-making style of organizations can be assessed by specifying the proportion of choices made in each of these three ways.

(a) By *oversight*. If a choice is activated when problems are attached to other choices and if there is energy available to make the new choice quickly, it will be made without any attention to existing problems and with a minimum of time and energy.

(b) By *flight*. In some cases, choices are associated with problems (unsuccessfully) for some time until a choice 'more attractive' to the problems comes along. The problems leave the choice, and thereby make it possible to make the decision. The decision resolves no problems (they having now attached themselves to a new choice).

(c) By *resolution*. Some choices resolve problems after some period of working on them. The length of time may vary greatly (depending on the number of problems). This is the familiar case that is implicit in most discussion of choice within organizations. (Cohen and March, 1974, p. 83)

Cohen and March identify several major properties of garbage can decision processes:

1. Decision-making by flight and oversight are central features of the process. Resolution of problems is uncommon except where flight is severely restricted or there are few problems under consideration.

2. The process is sensitive to variations in load. An increase in the load increases the use of flight and oversight:

> Problems are less likely to be solved, decision makers are likely to shift from one problem to another more frequently, choices are likely to take longer to make and be less likely to resolve problems. (Cohen and March, 1974, p. 85)

3. The decision-making process is interactive. Outcomes often depend on the particular time phasing of choices, problems and participant availability.

4. The system produces a queue of problems according to their importance. Early arriving and important problems are more likely to be solved than unimportant or late arriving problems, particularly when the load is heavy.

The major contribution of the garbage can model is that it uncouples problems and choices. The notion of decision-making as a rational process for achieving solutions to problems is supplanted by an uneasy mix of problems, solutions and participants from which decisions may eventually emerge. The garbage can model has a clear application to educational institutions where there are many participants with ready-made solutions to apply to different problems.

At Cambridgeshire College of Arts and Technology (CCAT) a group of staff were committed to the maintenance and development of part-time courses and pursued this 'solution' at various opportunities. In 1982 the National Advisory Board for Local Authority Higher Education (NAB) invited colleges to indicate priorities within their existing higher education courses on the assumption of a 10 per cent reduction in funding. The potential cuts package was discussed at the College's Academic Planning and Resources Committee where advocates of part-time provision sought to exclude those courses from the package. They were largely successful in that full-time courses took the brunt of the proposed cuts. The 'solution' of protecting and enhancing part-time courses was attached to the 'problem' of planning for a possible cut in resources. 'Staff who believe that part time vocational courses are at the heart of colleges like CCAT found in the NAB exercise a convenient vehicle for this view' (Bush and Goulding, 1984).

Ambiguity models: goals, structure, environment and leadership

Ambiguity models differ from all other approaches in stressing the problematic nature of *goals*. The other theories may emphasize the institution or the subunit or the individual but they all assume that objectives are clear at the levels identified. The distinctive quality of the ambiguity perspective is that purposes are regarded not only as vague and unclear but also as an inadequate guide to behaviour. Cohen *et al.* (1976, p. 37) claim:

> [. . .] events are not dominated by intention. The processes and the outcomes are likely to appear to have no close relation with the explicit intention of actors [. . .] intention is lost in context dependent flow of problems, solutions, people, and choice opportunities.

Ambiguity theorists argue that decision-making represents an opportunity for discovering goals rather than promoting policies based on existing objectives. The specific choice situation acts as a catalyst in helping individuals to clarify their preferences. 'Human choice behaviour is at least as much a process for discovering goals as for acting on them' (Cohen and March, 1974). Cuthbert (1984, p. 58) suggests that purposes in education may become clear only after the decision has been implemented and evaluated. The goals are speculative until they are confirmed by the outcomes of the choice:

[. . .] we can only discover after the event what the objectives of a choice were. At the time of making the choice we can only hypothesise possible goals of the choice. [. . .] Many staff development choices may be interpreted in these terms. The decision to support, for example, attendance at a course by a member of staff may be made with a view to several possible purposes: improving job-related skills or knowledge; personal development for the individual; as a reward for previous good behaviour; in the hope of generating some new (unspecified) approach to an organisational problem; and so on. Only after the event will one or more of these hypothetical goals (or some unconsidered alternative) be corroborated.

Ambiguity models regard organizational *structure* as problematic. Institutions are portrayed as aggregations of loosely coupled subunits so that structure may be both ambiguous and subject to change. In many educational organizations, and certainly in the larger schools and colleges, policy is determined primarily by committees rather than individuals. The various committees and working parties may be thought of as constituting the structure of the organization.

Enderud (1980) argues that organizational structure may be subject to a variety of interpretations because of the ambiguity and subunit autonomy that exists in many large and complex organizations. He points to a number of factors which influence interpretation:

1. Institutions usually classify responsibilities into decision areas which are then allocated to different bodies or individuals. An obvious example is the distinction made between the academic and pastoral structures in many secondary schools. However, these decision areas may not be delineated clearly or the topics treated within each area may overlap. A pupil's academic progress, for example, may be hampered by personal or domestic considerations:

   > The result is that a given decision may quite reasonably be subject to different classifications of decision area. This again means that the circle of participants who are to deal with the matter is also open to interpretation. (Enderud, 1980, p. 249).

2. Decisions may be classified also in ways other than by area. Issues may be major or minor, urgent or long term, administrative or political, and so on. These distinctions offer the same opportunities for different interpretations as exist with delineation by area.

3. Rules and regulations concerning the decision process within the formal structure may be unclear. The choice of rules for decision-making is often subject to *ad hoc* interpretation. The adoption of a voting process,

or an attempt to reach consensus or a proposal to defer a decision may be unpredictable and have a significant influence on the final outcome.

4. Rules and regulations may be disregarded in certain circumstances. Most organizational structures have elements designed to deal with emergencies or procedural conflicts. The formal structure may be circumvented to deal with particular occurrences where participants can agree on such practice.

A further source of ambiguity concerns the extent of participation within the organizational structure. Certain individuals within the institution have the right to participate in decision-making through their membership of committees and working parties. Cohen *et al.* (1976, p. 27) point out that committee membership is only the starting point for participation in decision making:

> Such rights are necessary, but not sufficient, for actual involvement in a decision. They can be viewed as invitations to participation. Invitations that may or may not be accepted.

A basic assumption of ambiguity models is that participation in decision-making is fluid as members underuse their decision rights. One consequence of such structural ambiguities is that decisions may be possible only where there are sufficient participants. Attempts to make decisions in situations where there is insufficient participation may founder at subsequent stages of the process.

The external *environment* is a source of ambiguity which adds to the unpredictability of organizations. Schools and colleges have a continuing existence only as long as they are able to satisfy the needs of their environments. So educational institutions have to be sensitive to the messages transmitted by external groups and individuals. Bell (1980, pp. 186–7) emphasizes that schools are increasingly dependent on elements within their environments:

> Perhaps it needs to be recognised more explicitly that organisations, including schools, sometimes operate in a complex and unstable environment over which they exert only modest control and which is capable of producing effects which penetrate the strongest and most selective of boundaries. [. . .] many schools are now unable to disregard pressures emanating from their wider environment. They are no longer able to respond to the uncertainty which such pressures often bring by attempting to buffer themselves against the unforeseen or by gaining control over the source of the uncertainty and thus restoring stability. The external pressures are, in many cases, too strong for that.

Ultimately institutions which fail to meet the requirements of their environments may suffer the penalty of contraction or closure. The demise of certain schools as a result of falling rolls may be regarded as a failure to satisfy market needs. Closure is often preceded by a period of decline as parents opt to send their children to other schools which are thought to be more suitable. One way of assessing these events is to view the unpopularity of schools as a product of their inability to interpret the wishes of the environment. A major difficulty is that the signals may be ambiguous. March and Olsen (1976, p. 18) discuss the reasons for this uncertainty:

> Environmental actions and events frequently are ambiguous. It is not clear what happened, or why it happened. Ambiguity may be inherent in the events, or be caused by the difficulties participants have in observing them. The complexity of, and change in, the environment often overpower our cognitive capacity. Furthermore, our interpretations are seldom based only on our own observations; they rely heavily on the interpretations offered by others. Our trust in the interpretations are clearly dependent on our trust in the interpretors. The degree of ambiguity will be strongly dependent upon the efficiency of the channels through which interpretations are transmitted.

Uncertainties about the requirements of the environment represent an additional source of ambiguity which interacts with the other unpredictable aspects of organizations to produce a confused pattern far removed from the clear, straightforward assumptions associated with the formal models. A turbulent environment combines with the internal ambiguities to ensure that management in education is a hazardous and changeable activity.

In a climate of ambiguity traditional ideas of *leadership* require modification. The unpredictable features of anarchic organizations create difficulties for the manager and suggest a different approach to the management of schools and colleges. According to Cohen and March (1974, pp. 195–203), leaders face four fundamental ambiguities:

1. There is an ambiguity of *purpose* because the goals of the organization are unclear. It is difficult to specify a set of clear, consistent goals which would receive the endorsement of members of the institution. Moreover, it may be impossible to infer a set of objectives from the activities of the organization. If there are no clear goals leaders have an inadequate basis for assessing the actions and achievements of the institution.
2. There is an ambiguity of *power* because it is difficult to make a clear assessment of the power of leaders. Heads and principals do possess authority arising from their position as the formal leaders of their

institutions. However, in an unpredictable setting formal authority is an uncertain guide to the power of leaders. Decisions emerge from a complex process of interaction. Leaders are participants in the process but their 'solutions' may not emerge as the preferred outcomes of the organisation.

3. There is an ambiguity of *experience* because in conditions of uncertainty leaders may not be able to learn from the consequences of their actions. In a straightforward situation leaders choose from a range of alternatives and assess the outcome in terms of the goals of the institution. This assessment then provides a basis for action in similar situations. In conditions of ambiguity, however, outcomes depend on factors other than the behaviour of the leaders. External changes occur and distort the situation so that experience becomes an unreliable guide to future action.

4. There is an ambiguity of *success* because it is difficult to measure the achievements of leaders. Heads and principals are usually appointed to these posts after successful careers as teachers and heads of departments. They have become familiar with success. However, the ambiguities of purpose, power and experience make it difficult for leaders to distinguish between success and failure.

Cohen and March (1974, p. 195) point to the problems for leaders faced with these uncertainties:

> These ambiguities are fundamental [. . .] because they strike at the heart of the usual interpretations of leadership. When purpose is ambiguous, ordinary theories of decision making and intelligence become problematic. When power is ambiguous, ordinary theories of social order and control become problematic. When experience is ambiguous, ordinary theories of learning and adaptation become problematic. When success is ambiguous, ordinary theories of motivation and personal pleasure become problematic.

These ambiguous features imply that leaders cannot control the institution in a manner suggested by the formal models. Rather they become facilitators of a complex decision-making process, creating opportunities for the discussion of problems, the participation of members and the exposition of solutions.

Two alternative leadership strategies are postulated for conditions of ambiguity. One stratagem involves a participative role for leaders to maximize their influence on policy. Cohen and March (1974) and March (1982) suggest the following approaches for the management of uncertainty.

1. Leaders should be ready to devote time to the process of decision-making. By taking the trouble to participate fully leaders are likely to be present when issues are finally resolved and will have the opportunity to influence the decision.
2. Leaders should be prepared to persist with those proposals which do not gain the initial support of groups within the institution. Issues are likely to surface at several forums and a negative reception at one setting may be reversed on another occasion when there may be different participants.
3. Leaders should facilitate the participation of groups and individuals likely to oppose the leader's proposals. Occasional participants tend to have aspirations which are out of touch with reality. Direct involvement in decision-making increases members' awareness of the ramifications of various courses of action. The inclusion of opponents at appropriate forums may lead to the modification or withdrawal of alternative ideas and allow the leader's plans to prosper.
4. Leaders should overload the system with ideas to ensure the success of some of the initiatives. When the organization has to cope with a surfeit of issues it is likely that some of the proposals will succeed even if others fall by the wayside.

These tactical manoeuvres may appear rather cynical and they have certain similarities with the political models discussed in Chapter 5. The alternative approach is for leaders to forsake direct involvement in the policy-making process and to concentrate on structural and personnel matters. Attention to the formal structure enables leaders to influence the framework of decision-making. In deciding where issues should be discussed there is an effect on the outcome of those discussions.

In this view leaders are urged to pay careful attention to the selection and deployment of staff. If heads or principals recruit teachers who share their educational philosophies then it is likely that their preferred solutions will become school or college policy. The structural and personnel aspects of management can overlap. Heads may encourage like-minded staff to join committees and working parties to improve prospects of favourable outcomes. 'These policy recommendations amount to unobtrusive management in the extreme. The emphasis is on structural design and personnel selection, rather than tactical machinations' (Padgett, 1980).

Both these strategies suggest that leaders in ambiguous situations should proceed by stealth rather than overt proclamation of particular policies. As

Baldridge *et al.* (1978, p. 26) point out, the management of uncertainty requires somewhat different qualities from the management of bureaucracies:

> In such fluid circumstances [. . .] leaders serve primarily as catalysts. They do not so much lead the institution as they channel its activities in subtle ways. They do not command, they negotiate. They do not plan comprehensively, they try to nudge problems together with preexisting solutions. They are not heroic leaders, they are facilitators of an ongoing process.

The limitations of ambiguity models

Ambiguity models introduce some important dimensions into our consideration of management in education. The concepts of problematic goals, unclear technology and fluid participation are valuable additions to our understanding of organizations. Most schools and colleges possess these features to a greater or lesser extent. So ambiguity perspectives can be regarded primarily as analytical or descriptive approaches rather than normative theories. They claim to mirror reality rather than suggesting that organizations *should* operate as anarchies. Cohen and March (1974, p. 91) admit that their garbage can model has limitations while proclaiming its relevance to many organisations:

> We acknowledge immediately that no real system can be fully characterised in this way. Nonetheless, the simulated organisations exhibit behaviours that can be observed some of the time in almost all organisations and frequently in some.

Ambiguity models have four significant weaknesses.

1. It is difficult to reconcile ambiguity perspectives with the customary structures and processes of schools and colleges. Participants may move in and out of decision-making situations but the policy framework remains intact and has a continuing influence on the outcome of discussions. Specific goals may be unclear but teaching staff usually understand and accept the broad aims of education. The ambiguity model advances some important ideas but it falls short of a complete theory of educational organizations. Indeed, in some ways it 'seems curiously divorced from the familiar world of hierarchical authority, organisational differentiation, standard operating procedures, and centralisation policy known to us all' (Padgett, 1980).

2. Ambiguity models exaggerate the degree of unpredictability in educational institutions. Schools and colleges have a number of predictable

features which serve to clarify the responsibilities of their members. Students, pupils and staff are expected to behave in accordance with standard rules and procedures. The timetable regulates the location and movement of all members of the institution. There is often a defined syllabus to guide the classroom activities of teachers and pupils. Staff are aware of the accountability patterns, with teachers responsible to heads of departments, and ultimately to heads and principals for the satisfactory performance of their duties.

The predictability of schools and colleges is reinforced by the professional socialization which occurs during teacher training and the early years of practice. Teachers assimilate the expected patterns of behaviour and reproduce them in their professional lives. Socialization thus serves to reduce uncertainty and unpredictability in education. All these considerations suggest that educational institutions are rather more predictable than the ambiguity perspective implies. As Baldridge *et al.* (1978) point out, 'the term organised anarchy may seem overly colourful, suggesting more confusion, disarray, and conflict than is really present'.

3. Ambiguity models are not well suited to stable organizations or to any institutions during periods of stability. Turner (1977) argues that the degree of predictability in schools depends crucially on the extent and nature of relationships with the external environment. Where institutions are able to maintain relatively impervious boundaries they can exert strong control over their own activities and processes. Perhaps a few selective schools and ancient universities are in this position in the 1980s. The anarchic metaphor would be inappropriate for such ordered institutions.

The ambiguity perspective is relevant to those institutions which are subject to changes imposed by an increasingly turbulent environment. Falling rolls, expenditure cuts, youth unemployment, curricular and examination reforms and parental expectations are some of the external pressures on our schools and colleges. These sources of instability help to create unpredictable conditions, which in turn justify the use of ambiguity models in education. A cry which is heard increasingly from heads and other staff is a plea for a period of stability to enable their schools to absorb changes. Such appeals are futile in the context of rapid and multiple change but emphasize the discomfort engendered by periods of uncertainty. The applicability of ambiguity models thus depends crucially on the degree of turbulence in the environment.

4. Ambiguity models offer little practical guidance to leaders in educational institutions. As Cuthbert (1984) suggests, 'purposeful management is

difficult to reconcile with problematic goals, unclear technology, and fluid participation'. While formal models emphasize the head's leading role in policy-making and democratic models stress the importance of team work, ambiguity models can offer nothing more tangible than unobtrusive management. Even Cohen and March (1974) concede that 'the garbage can process does not do a particularly good job of resolving problems'. The analytical framework presented by ambiguity theorists includes many important ideas but this line of theory has yet to develop to the stage where it gives verifiable advice about the management of education in conditions of uncertainty and unpredictability.

Despite these limitations ambiguity models make a valuable contribution to our understanding of the operation of educational institutions. The emphasis on the unpredictability of organizations is a significant counter to the view that problems can be solved by a rational process. The notion of managers making a considered choice from a range of alternatives depends crucially on their ability to predict the consequences of a particular action. The edifice of the formal models is shaken by the recognition that conditions in schools and colleges may be too uncertain to allow an informed choice among alternatives. The ambiguity perspective is certainly partial but, as Baldridge *et al.* (1978, p. 27) demonstrate, it offers useful insights into the nature of school and college management:

> In many ways the organized anarchy image is an exceptionally strong and persuasive concept. It breaks through much traditional formality that surrounds discussions of decision making. The imagery of organised anarchy helps capture the spirit of the confused organisational dynamics in academic institutions: unclear goals, unclear technologies, and environmental vulnerability. [. . .] the term helps to expand our conceptions, dislodge the bureaucracy image, and suggest a looser, more fluid kind of organisation.

References

Baldridge, J.V., Curtis, D.V., Ecker, G. and Riley, G.L. (1978) *Policy Making and Effective Leadership*, Jossey Bass, San Francisco

Bell, L.A. (1980) The school as an organisation: a re-appraisal, *British Journal of Sociology of Education*, Vol. 1, No. 2, pp. 183–192.

Bush, T. and Goulding, S. (1984) *Cambridgeshire College of Arts and Technology: facing the cuts*, E324 Management in Post Compulsory Education, Block 3, Part 4, Open University Press, Milton Keynes.

Cohen, M.D. and March, J.G. (1986) *Leadership and Ambiguity: the American College President*, The Harvard Business School Press, Boston MA. (First published 1974 by McGraw-Hill, New York)

Cohen, M.D., March, J.G. and Olsen, J.P. (1976) People, problems, solutions and the ambiguity of relevance. In J.G. March and J.P. Olsen, *Ambiguity and Choice in Organisations*, Universitetsforlaget, Bergen.

Cuthbert, R. (1984) *The Management Process*, E324 Management in Post Compulsory Education, Block 3, Part 2, Open University Press, Milton Keynes.

Enderud, H. (1980) Administrative leadership in organised anarchies, *International Journal of Institutional Management in Higher Education*, Vol. 4, No. 3, pp. 235–253.

March, J.G. (1982) Theories of choice and making decisions, *Society*, Vol. 20, No. 1, copyright © by Transaction Inc. Published by permission of Transaction Inc.

March, J.G. and Olsen, J.P. (1976) Organisational choice under ambiguity. In J.G. March and J.P. Olsen *Ambiguity and Choice in Organisations*, Universitetsforlaget, Bergen.

Noble, T. and Pym, B. (1970) Collegial authority and the receding locus of power, *British Journal of Sociology*, Vol. 21, pp. 431–445.

Padgett, J.F. (1980) Managing garbage can hierarchies, *Administrative Science Quarterly*, Vol. 25, No. 4, pp. 583–604.

Turner, C. (1977) Organising educational institutions as anarchies, *Educational Administration*, Vol. 5, No. 2, pp. 6–12.

Weick, K.E. (1976) Educational organisations as loosely coupled systems, *Administrative Science Quarterly*, Vol. 21, No. 1, pp. 1–19.

CHAPTER 8

CONCLUSION: TOWARDS A COMPREHENSIVE MODEL

The models compared

The five perspectives discussed in this book represent different ways of looking at educational institutions. They are windows which afford a view of life in schools or colleges. Each portrayal offers valuable insights into the nature of management in education but none provides a complete picture. The five approaches are all valid analyses but their relevance depends on the situation and the type of institution concerned. In certain circumstances one model may appear to be applicable while another perspective may seem more appropriate in a different setting. There is no single approach capable of presenting a total framework for our understanding of educational institutions, as Baldridge *et al.* (1978, p. 28) demonstrate:

> [. . .] the search for an all-encompassing model is simplistic, for no one model can delineate the intricacies of decision processes in complex organisations such as universities and colleges [. . .] there is a pleasant parsimony about having a single model that summarises a complicated world for us. This is not bad except when we allow our models to blind us to important features of the organisation.

The five models differ along crucial dimensions but taken together they provide a comprehensive appraisal of the nature of management in educational institutions. We have chosen to emphasize four main aspects of organizations and it is useful to reconsider these elements in comparing the five perspectives.

There are significant differences in the assumptions made about the *goals* of educational organizations. Formal models aver that objectives are set at the institutional level. It is thought that goals are determined by senior staff and the support of other teachers is taken for granted. The activities of schools and colleges are then evaluated in the light of these official purposes.

Democratic models suggest that members of an organization agree on its goals. These approaches have a harmony bias in that they assume that it is always possible for staff to reach agreement based on common values. Unlike formal perspectives the objectives are not imposed from above but emerge from a participative process.

Political models differ from both the formal and democratic models in stressing the goals of subunits or departments rather than institutional objectives. Moreover there is conflict as groups seek to promote their purposes. Goals are unstable as subunits engage in negotiation and alliances form and break down.

Subjective models emphasize the goals of individuals rather than institutional or group purposes. The concept of organizational objectives is supplanted by the view that individuals have personal aims. Schools and colleges are regarded as the subjective creations of the people within them and the only reality is their individual perceptions of the organization. Goals attributed to organizations are thought to be the purposes of the most powerful individuals within them.

Ambiguity models claim that goals are problematic. While other perspectives assume that objectives are clear at institutional, group or individual levels the ambiguity approach suggests that goals are opaque. Objectives are also regarded as an unreliable guide to behaviour. In this view it is mistaken to regard policies or events as a corollary of the goals of the institution.

The notion of organizational *structure* takes on different meanings within the various perspectives. Formal and democratic models regard structures as objective realities. Individuals hold defined positions in the organization and working relationships are assumed to be strongly influenced by these official positions. Formal models treat structures as hierarchical with decisions being passed down from the leader. Democratic models present structures as lateral with all members taking part in the decision process.

Political models portray structure as one of the unstable and conflictual elements of the institution. The design of the structure is thought to reflect the interests to be served by the organization. The elements within the structure may become the settings for conflict between interest groups anxious to promote their policy objectives.

Subjective models regard organizational structure as a product of the relationships of individuals rather than a fixed entity which constrains the behaviour of its participants. The interaction of members of the organization is reflected in the structure which is valid only as long as it accurately represents those relationships.

Ambiguity models assume that organizational structure is one of the problematic aspects of institutions. Structure is ambiguous because of the uncertain relationships between loosely coupled subunits. The relevance of structure may be further compromised by the fluid participation of members in committees and other forums.

Relations with external groups are an increasingly important consideration for educational institutions if they are to survive and prosper. These links with the *environment* are portrayed in very different ways by the various perspectives. Some of the formal approaches tend to regard schools and colleges as 'closed systems' relatively impervious to outside influences. Other formal theories typify educational organizations as 'open systems', responding to the needs of their communities and building a positive image to attract new clients.

Democratic models tend to be inadequate in explaining relationships with the environment. Policy is thought to be determined within a participatory framework making it difficult to locate responsibility for decisions. Heads may be held accountable for outcomes which do not enjoy their personal support, leading to confusion among external groups and stress for the leader. Democratic approaches gloss over this difficulty by the unrealistic assumption that heads are always in agreement with decisions and are thus expected to be in a good position to explain them to outside bodies.

Political models tend to portray relationships with the environment as unstable. External bodies are regarded as interest groups participating in the complex bargaining process which is thought to be characteristic of decision-making in education. Internal and external groups may form alliances to press for the adoption of certain policies. Interaction with the environment is seen as a key aspect of an essentially political decision process.

In subjective models the environment is treated primarily as a source of the meanings placed on events by people within the organization. Individuals are thought to interpret situations in different ways and these variations are attributed to differences in the backgrounds of, and external influences upon, participants.

Ambiguity models regard the environment as a source of uncertainty which contributes to the unpredictability of organizations. The signals from outside groups are often unclear and contradictory, adding to the confusion inside schools and colleges. Interpretation of messages from a turbulent environment may be difficult thus further emphasizing the ambiguity of the decision process.

The styles of *leadership* inevitably reflect the particular features of the diverse models of management. Within formal perspectives it is thought that the official leader has a key role in decision-making, determining goals and formulating policy. Heads and principals are located at the apex of a hierarchy and they are acknowledged as the leaders both inside and outside the institution. It is assumed that the leader possesses much of the organization's power.

In democratic models policies are thought to emerge from a complex process of discussion at committees and other settings, both formal and informal. Influence is distributed widely within the institution and the leader is one participant in a collegial style of decision-making. Heads are assumed to have the prime responsibility for the promotion of consensus among their fellow professionals. A hierarchical approach is regarded as inappropriate for participative organizations.

Political models assume that leaders are active participants in the process of bargaining and negotiation which characterizes decision-making in organizations. Heads and principals have significant resources of power which they are able to deploy in support of their interests and objectives. Leaders may also mediate between groups in order to develop acceptable policy outcomes.

Subjective models de-emphasize the concept of leadership preferring to stress the personal attributes of individuals rather than their official positions in the organization. Leaders are assumed to have their own values and objectives which necessarily influence their interpretation of events. Heads and principals may be able to exert control over colleagues by enunciating institutional policies in line with their own personal interests and requiring the compliance of staff with these interpretations.

Ambiguity models stress the uncertainty facing leaders and the difficulties associated with the management of unpredictability. There are two schools of thought about the most appropriate leadership strategies for conditions of ambiguity. One mode is to engage in various tactical machinations in an approach similar to those adopted by political leaders. The alternative stance is to adopt an unobtrusive style with an emphasis on personnel and structural issues. Here the leader sets the framework for decision-making but avoids direct involvement in the policy-making process.

Elements of management	Type of model				
	Formal	Democratic	Political	Subjective	Ambiguity
Level at which goals are determined	Institutional	Institutional	Subunit	Individual	Unclear
Process by which goals are determined	Set by leaders	Agreement	Conflict	Problematic May be imposed by leaders	Unpredictable
Relationship between goals and decisions	Decisions based on goals	Decisions based on agreed goals	Decisions based on goals of dominant coalitions	Individual behaviour based on personal objectives	Decisions unrelated to goals
Nature of decision process	Rational	Collegial	Political	Personal	Garbage can
Nature of structure	Objective reality Hierarchical	Objective reality Lateral	Setting for subunit conflict	Constructed through human interaction	Problematic
Links with environment	May be 'closed' or 'open' Head accountable	Accountability blurred by shared decision making	Unstable External bodies portrayed as interest groups	Source of individual meanings	Source of uncertainty
Style of leadership	Head establishes goals and initiates policy	Head seeks to promote consensus	Head is both participant and mediator	Problematic May be perceived as a form of control	May be tactical or unobtrusive

Figure 8.1 Comparison of five models of management

The five perspectives differ significantly in the ways in which they treat goals, structure, environment and leadership. There are also notable variations in respect of other aspects of institutional management. The major features of the five models are identified in Figure 8.1.

Applying the models to schools and colleges

The five perspectives represent conceptually distinct approaches to the management of educational institutions. However, it is rare for a single model to capture the reality of management in any particular school or college. Rather aspects of several perspectives are present in different proportions of each institution. The validity of the various models depends on five overlapping considerations:

1. The *size* of the institution is a key influence on the nature of management structure and process. A small two teacher primary school necessarily operates very differently from a large multi-department polytechnic. The two primary teachers are likely to determine policy by informal agreement while the head is acknowledged as the official leader by external groups and individuals. It may be appropriate to regard the management of such schools as comprising elements of both the democratic and formal models.

In large and complex institutions such as polytechnics and colleges there are numerous decision points leading to the development of alternative power centres. Staff may owe their first loyalty to their discipline and their department. These subunits compete for the resources they require to advance their objectives in a process encapsulated by the political model. In certain circumstances the situation may be so fluid that the ambiguity perspective may appear to be appropriate.

2. The nature of the *organizational structure* may have a significant impact on the ways in which schools and colleges are managed. Heads who establish participative machinery may be motivated by a desire to involve professional colleagues in decision-making. The intention then is to create a democratic framework for policy formulation. However, the introduction of committees and working parties also provides a focus for political behaviour. Interest groups seek representation on these bodies and engage in bargaining and alliance building. The democratic and political dimensions are both enhanced by the introduction of a participative structure while the formal perspective necessarily has a reduced validity in these circumstances.

3. The nature of the management process depends on the amount of *time* which participants are able and willing to devote to the wider organizational and managerial aspects of their work. In the primary sector teachers have full-time classroom responsibilities and only the head is available to deal with management issues during the school day. This fact suggests that the formal model is likely to apply to most primary schools. In secondary schools, and particularly in post school institutions, staff have periods of nonteaching time which they may be able to devote to committee work or to other managerial activities. The existence of this 'free' time is an important precondition for the development of democratic and political approaches.

The validity of democratic models may be circumscribed by the reluctance of staff to participate in decision-making. Where teachers opt out of committees and working parties they may be signalling their indifference to a participative approach. This tends to reduce the appropriateness of democratic perspectives and may also limit the applicability of political models. Where individuals ascribe different meanings to structural devices like committees, the subjective approach may appear to be particularly relevant.

4. The *availability of resources* is likely to play a part in determining the relevance of the various models. In periods of expansion it may be possible to adopt a rational approach to the distribution of resources or to rely on a collegial stance. When resources are limited departments face the possibility of cutbacks in staff levels or reductions in capitation or equipment. Such threats to the viability of academic units are likely to lead to these groups seeking to defend their interests. Committees and working parties may begin to resemble political arenas as subunits seek to retain existing resource levels. Davies and Morgan (1983, p. 164) chart the shift from formal and democratic approaches to a political perspective as resources dwindle:

> As long as powerful individuals and groups received what they perceived to be reasonable shares of expanding resources, the core organisational coalitions were maintained in relative harmony [. . .] As resources to meet the policy commitments and funding demands of competing organisational groups have diminished, institutional administrators have experienced an increased level of conflict.

5. The nature and rate of *change in the environment* are additional considerations which impinge on the process of management inside schools and colleges. In periods of stability institutions may be able to adopt formal

or democratic approaches to the internal operation of educational institutions. When the environment is turbulent and unpredictable the ambiguity model may be particularly appropriate. Doubts over levels of funding and the size of pupil or student intakes are major sources of instability in the 1980s leading to confusion within institutions.

It may be possible to conclude that small schools are correctly typified as formal or democratic organizations, especially in periods of stability. Equally, large, multipurpose colleges undergoing rapid change may be explained best by political or ambiguity models. The large number of schools lying between these two extremes are likely to possess features of all five models which vary in significance from time to time and from one activity to another. Adherents of the subjective model would add that much depends on the perceptions of individual staff and pupils.

> Each set of models shades into the next because each model is necessarily partial [. . .] What is important will vary from one situation to the next, and from one observer or participant to another [. . .] Usefulness is not an objective criterion; it depends on the attitudes, values, beliefs, skills and experiences of the user. (Cuthbert, 1984, p. 62)

Attempts at synthesis

Each of the five models presented in this volume offers valid insights into the nature of management in schools and colleges. Yet all the perspectives are limited in that they do not give a complete picture of educational institutions. Rather they turn the spotlight on particular aspects of the organization and consequently leave other features in the shade. Some writers argue that it is possible to obtain a comprehensive appraisal of organizations by using elements from some or all of the models. Ellstrom (1983, p. 236) makes the case for such a synthesis:

> [. . .] each model emphasises certain variables, while others are deemphasised or ignored. Consequently, each model can be expected to give only partial understanding of the organisational reality. [. . .] it might be possible to obtain a more comprehensive understanding of organisations by integrating the [. . .] models into an overarching framework.
>
> A basic assumption [. . .] is the idea of complementarity [. . .] That is, the models are viewed as compatible, rather than as mutually exclusive alternatives.

Enderud (1980) and Davies and Morgan (1983) have developed integrative models incorporating ambiguity, political, collegial and formal perspectives. These syntheses are based on the assumption that policy formation proceeds through four distinct phases which all require adequate time if the decision is to be successful. Attempts by leaders to omit certain stages or to hurry issues through the process may lead to subsequent breakdown or create the necessity for a loopback to earlier phases.

The models posit an initial period of high ambiguity as problems, solutions and participants interact at appropriate choice opportunities. This anarchic phase serves to identify the issues and acts as a preliminary sifting mechanism. If conducted properly it should lead to an initial coupling of problems with potential solutions.

The output of the ambiguous period is regarded as the input to the political phase. This stage is characterized by bargaining and negotiations and usually involves relatively few participants in small, closed committees. The outcome is likely to be a broad measure of agreement on possible solutions.

In the third collegial phase the participants committed to the proposed solution attempt to persuade less active members to accept the compromise reached during the political stage. The solutions are tested against criteria of acceptability and feasibility and may result in minor changes. Eventually this process should lead to agreed policy outcomes and a degree of commitment to the decision.

The final phase is the formal or bureaucratic stage during which agreed policy may be subject to modification in the light of administrative considerations. The outcome of this period is a policy which is both legitimate and operationally satisfactory. The Davies and Morgan (1983) version of the model is shown as Figure 8.2.

Enderud (1980, p. 241) emphasizes that the significance of each phase varies according to the different perceptions of participants as well as the nature of the issue:

> With its four phases, the model [. . .] reflects a mix of different realities in [. . .] decision making – an anarchistic, a political, a collegial and a bureaucratic reality – which may all be part of any one joint decision process. This composite picture will be one of the reasons why different participants often can interpret the same decision as largely anarchic, political, collegial or bureaucratic, according to the phase which is most visible to them, because of their own participation or for other reasons.

Although Enderud acknowledges that the individual interpretations of

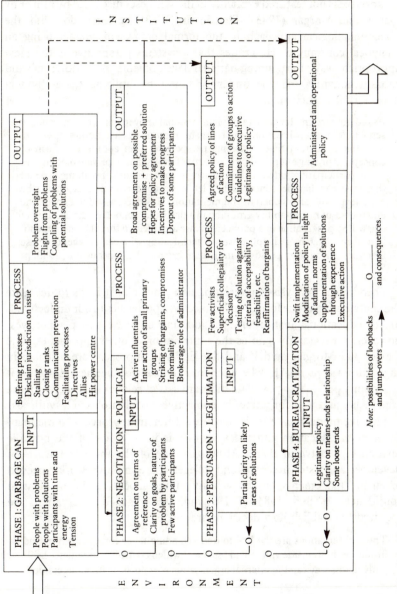

Figure 8.2 A four phase model of policy formation (from Davies and Morgan, 1983)

ENVIRONMENT · INSTITUTION

PHASE 1: GARBAGE CAN

INPUT
- People with problems
- People with solutions
- Participants with time and energy
- Tension

PROCESS
Buffering processes
- Disclaim jurisdiction on issue
- Stalling
- Closing ranks
- Communication prevention
- Facilitating processes
- Directives
- Allies
- Hit power centre

OUTPUT
- Problem oversight
- Flight from problems
- Coupling of problems with potential solutions

PHASE 2: NEGOTIATION + POLITICAL

INPUT
- Agreement on terms of reference
- Clarity on goals, nature of problem by participants
- Few active participants

PROCESS
- Active influentials
- Interaction of small primary groups
- Striking of bargains, compromises
- Informality
- Brokerage role of administrator

OUTPUT
- Broad agreement on possible compromise + preferred solution
- Hopes for policy agreement
- Incentives to make progress
- Dropout of some participants

PHASE 3: PERSUASION + LEGITIMATION

INPUT
- Partial clarity on likely areas of solutions

PROCESS
- Few activists
- Superficial collegiality for 'decision'
- Testing of solution against criteria of acceptability, feasibility, etc.
- Reaffirmation of bargains

OUTPUT
- Agreed policy of lines of action
- Commitment of groups to action
- Guidelines to executive
- Legitimacy of policy

PHASE 4: BUREAUCRATIZATION

INPUT
- Legitimate policy
- Clarity on means-ends relationship
- Some loose ends

PROCESS
- Swift implementation
- Modification of policy in light of admin. norms
- Supplementation of solutions through experience
- Executive action

OUTPUT
- Administered and operational policy

Note: possibilities of loopbacks O and jump-overs and consequences.

participants may influence the visibility of the models the subjective perspective is not featured explicitly in the syntheses discussed by him or by Davies and Morgan (1983). Theodossin (1983), however, does link the phenomenological approach to the formal or systems model using an analytical continuum. He argues that a systems perspective is the most appropriate way of explaining national developments while individual and subunit activities may be understood best by utilizing the individual meanings of participants:

> Asked to account for and to explain national movements (e.g. secondary school comprehensivisation, the reorganisation of teacher training), we are more likely to find that a systems perspective is an appropriate form of conceptual organisation: to think in terms of thousands of private biographies of the participating individuals is clearly to concern oneself with more detail than one can handle conceptually, let alone collect, and to segment the experience into an incoherent fragmentation. However, asked to explain the emergence of mixed-ability grouping in a particular school, or the creation of a new BSc programme in a polytechnic, we are likely to find the phenomenological approach more helpful: we are here dealing with change agents whose activities spring from personal, individual experience. (Theodossin, 1983, p. 88)

Theodossin's analysis is interesting and plausible. It helps to delineate the contribution of the formal and subjective approaches to our understanding of educational institutions. In focusing on these two perspectives, however, it necessarily ignores the contribution of other approaches. The Davies and Morgan model, and the Enderud approach, are valuable in suggesting a sequential link between four of the major theories. However, it is certainly possible to postulate different sets of relationships between the approaches and to incorporate the subjective model into such a synthesis.

The five models serve to demonstrate different approaches to the management of education and the syntheses indicate a few of the possible relationships between them. Although some of the theories have been developed and tested in schools and colleges, more empirical work is needed to enable judgements on the validity of the models to be made with confidence. As Bell (1984, p. 199) indicates, detailed observations are required to establish how decisions are made:

> These observations are the key to understanding those forces of power and influence, both inside and outside schools, which control and regulate them. Only in this way can the internal organisation of schools be fully understood.

References

Baldridge, J. V., Curtis, D.V., Ecker, G. and Riley, G.L. (1978) *Policy Making and Effective Leadership*, Jossey Bass, San Francisco

Bell, L. (1984) The sociology of school organisation: impossible or irrelevant?, *British Journal of Sociology of Education*, Vol. 5. No. 2, pp. 187–204.

Cuthbert, R. (1984) *The Management Process*, E324 Management in Post Compulsory Education, Block 3, Part 2, Open University Press, Milton Keynes

Davies, J.L. and Morgan, A.W. (1983) Management of higher education in a period of contraction and uncertainty. In O. Boyd-Barrett, T. Bush, J. Goodey, J. McNay and M. Preedy (eds). *Approaches to Post School Management*, Harper and Row, London

Ellstrom, P.E (1983) Four faces of educational organisations, *Higher Education*, Vol. 12, pp. 231–241

Enderud, J. (1980) Administrative leadership in organised anarchies, *International Journal of Institutional Management in Higher Education*, Vol. 4, No. 3, pp. 235–253

Theodossin, E. (1983) Theoretical perspectives on the management of planned educational change, *British Educational Research Journal*, Vol. 9, No. 1, pp 81–90.

"Figure 8.1 has certain similarities with Cuthbert's (1984) tabular representation of five models using the criteria noted on page 18 above."

AUTHOR INDEX

SUBJECT INDEX